BEST OF
GREEN SPACE
30 Years of Composted Columns
Duane Campbell

sketches by Betty Mackey

B. B. Mackey Books
Wayne, PA 19087

Photography: Duane Campbell and Betty Mackey. Line drawings: Betty Mackey and historical sources.
ISBN 978-1-893443-16-7

Thank you to all those newspapers who have endured me over the decades. DC

Library of Congress Cataloging-in-Publication Data

Campbell, Duane, 1942-
  Best of Green space : 30 years of composted columns / by Duane Campbell ; sketches by Betty Mackey. -- 1st ed.
      p. cm.
  Includes bibliographical references and index.
  ISBN 978-1-893443-16-7 (alk. paper)
  1.   Gardening--Anecdotes. 2.   Newspapers--Sections, columns, etc.--Gardening.   I. Mackey, Betty. II. Green space (Newspaper column) III. Title.
  SB455.C32 2010
  635--dc22

                                        2010002749

For more information about this and other books published by B. B. Mackey Books, contact

B. B. Mackey Books   www.mackeybooks.com
P. O. Box 475   betty@mackeybooks.com
Wayne, PA 19087

for Deidre and Megan

becoming gardeners

CONTENTS

PREFACE

Over the decades, a number of people have said I should write a book. Two of them were not even blood relatives.

The thought had appeal. There were things I didn't have room to say in a newspaper column, there were things I didn't say very well that have made me cringe for years, there were things I have learned since writing some columns. It would be nice to revise and extend like our congressmen, to say what I should have said if I had known better.

I demurred for several reasons. First, I really like writing for newspapers. Newspaper editors have a deadline only hours away. They meet it, go to bed, and wake up with another deadline only hours away. They don't have time to pick at every dot and tittle. The garden piece is a dozen column inches they don't have to fuss over; paste it into the page and move on to something important.

Second, a book is a lot of work. A friend gave me a plaque that occupies a prominent place in my garden: "Work is for people who don't know how to garden."

Even so, I started a book. Several times. But I would wake at night drenched in sweat with nightmares about a cavernous room filled with tables as far as the eye could see, each table piled high with remaindered books, each book with my picture on the back.

The third reason is that potential publishers apparently had the same nightmare.

As a gardener I should have an intimate understanding of putting in huge effort with no results, but writing a book involved no sunshine on my back, no smell of rich earth in my nostrils, no flowers, no garden fresh vegetables, no upside.

Garden books that sell are glossy and full of pictures, usually of gardens the author had nothing to do with. I work with words, black text on white paper. The occasional Barnes and Noble customer who stumbles by accident into the garden section would

pick it up, fan through the pages, and seeing nothing but print, put it back down.

But technology's invidious advance squelched my nightmarish excuse. Print On Demand processes meant that it was no longer necessary to do an initial press run of 5,000 copies, no remainder tables, no attic filled with heavy boxes. Order a book, and instead of rummaging through a warehouse with a forklift, the publisher rummages through a hard drive with a mouse and the book instantly pops out of a 21st century printing press, just like your digital snapshots at a five minute photo booth.

It is traditional in these introductions to give proper thanks to the author's mother, who inspired his love of plants. My mother grew African violets. This was in the 1950s when there were two kinds, dingy pink ones and dingy blue ones. She had a hundred of each, and I had to water them. I left home with a love of gardening akin to the love Tom Sawyer had for fences.

Skip a decade, during which I went to college, defended my country against Communism as a second tenor, and married my high school sweetheart. After the pseudo-military experience, Judi and I lived in Europe for several years in a plantless apartment, and then, like salmon swimming upstream, returned home to spawn.

After living in a country where every Hausfrau had flowers stuffed in the two-foot front yard and spilling out of window boxes, we were faced with a barren American suburban landscape. Gardens we had never particularly noticed we suddenly missed. We needed flowers, not yews, and the only way to get them was to grow them, so I became a gardener of sorts.

I beat the gardening craze that swept the country in the 1970s by about two weeks. This slight edge made me the local expert, and neighbors started asking my advice. For the past three decades I have been giving it in a column, *Green Space*, which runs weekly in newspapers in the Northeast, and for a while on a radio show that did pretty well until the station realized they could run syndicated political talk shows for free.

Along the way I became a Master Gardener in two states, then a teacher of Master Gardeners. I taught gardening courses at a community college, judged gardens for the Pennsylvania Horticultural Society, spoke to more groups than I can remember, and picked up some national awards.

As impressive as this may sound, at least the way I relate it, I am not an expert. Experts are university professors who get grants and run controlled studies with herds of slave labor grad students to do the actual work. I am a home gardener with dirty hands, a generalist with some small knowledge in most areas and maybe a bit more in ornamentals, container growing, and indoor plants. I write about what I know from experience, not about what I've read in books.

Through the decades I have learned more, usually by screwing up, and I managed to stay two weeks ahead of my audience.

So here I should thank those two people who encouraged me and are not blood relatives, and I do, but not by name. They would probably like to remain blameless.

JANUARY

Resolutions

It's time for the dismal chore of making New Year's resolutions. The positive slant is that this is a new beginning. The truth is that we are making a list of all those things that we habitually screw up. I have a ritual. I pull a yellowed paper from my desk, unfold it—careful not to crack the brittle creases—read the list put together years ago, and resolve once again to do them. Really try this time. Honest.

Some people make new resolutions each year, but I don't need to. I have plenty left over. Don't tell me you've never recycled a New Year's resolution.

One leftover is stacked on my desk right now—a lamp-high pile of various loose leaf, spiral, or fancy garden journals, all with the first few pages meticulously filled in but otherwise empty. If you want to know about my gardening in the first couple of weeks of any January, back to the early 1970s, I can tell you. Don't ask me about June, though.

Another I have actually done, but I need to remind myself every January. Get seed starting mix.

Seed starting mix is a sterile soil mix that is more finely sifted than normal potting soil. In recent years it has sold out early, gone before I actually need it. So as soon as it appears on store shelves, while the last plastic Christmas trees linger at 90 percent off, I get my supply.

I resolve not to order more seeds than I can use. Yeah, well. Let's move on.

This year I resolve to test suspect seeds at least a month before planting time. I keep seeds, sometimes for years, and their viability dwindles with age, sometimes down to nothing. It's a good idea to find out before time to start them for real. Too many years I have not had some treasured plant in my garden because old seed didn't germinate.

11

The process is simple. Count out ten seeds, lay them along the edge of a paper towel, and roll it up tightly. Mark the name of the seed and the date on the towel, wet it well, drain, and put it in a Ziploc bag in a warm spot.

In a couple of weeks, unwrap them and check for a radicle, the beginning of a root, emerging. If none has, but some seeds have swelled, put them back in the baggie for another week or two and check again. The number of seeds that have sprouted times ten gives your germination percentage. If it is zero, there is still time to get new seeds.

This must be done well before you would normally start planting seeds, which brings me to my next resolution. Make a schedule. I used to do this routinely every spring, but I slacked off because I thought I knew what I was doing. I didn't.

Different seeds get planted at different times depending on how long they need to grow to transplant size and when they can go out in the garden. Melons, for instance, only need four weeks to transplant and go out the first week of June, after the ground is well warmed. Onions, on the other hand, need eight weeks and go out in April.

Using a free wall calendar from the bank or the insurance company, I prominently mark the average last frost date, early in the second week of May for me. That's a starting point.

Just about every garden magazine at the checkout this time of year has a chart telling you when transplants go out and how long they take. Tomatoes, for example, need eight weeks and go out after the last frost. So take the last frost date, move your game piece ahead one week to be safe, count back eight weeks, and write t-o-m-a-t-o.

For the adventurous, count back another four weeks and write "tomato" again. This is the early, and risky, first planting. You can warm the soil with plastic mulch—black or, better still for warming, clear—and protect the plants with water towers or floating row cover. Or you can just put them out and hope the frost date is wrong this year.

Peppers take longer than tomatoes. Lettuce and Chinese cabbage and cole crops are ready in six weeks, but they go out much earlier in spring. It's all too much for my mind to keep straight, so I will write it all down on the calendar. Now. In January, when I have the time.

Next resolution: Remember to look at the calendar.

Winter Garden

You know what an oxymoron is, right? A phrase that is ironically self-contradictory, like jumbo shrimp or accordion music. Or winter garden.

Gardening magazines this time of year are full of illustrated stories about winter gardens. If you look carefully at the photos, you will notice that they are all taken outdoors. I don't go outdoors in winter. It's cold. And I've put on a few pounds, so my galoshes don't fit.

Therefore my rule for summer landscaping goes double for winter. Triple maybe. Plan your garden from your window. In summer I recommend that you pay special attention to the view out the windows. In winter that advice becomes imperative: Don't bother with anything you can't see from inside.

Some people think winter garden decor is neat burlap boxes around their evergreens. What's the point? The whole idea of evergreens is that you have something green in winter, not something square and brown. If you are saving them for summer, let's be honest: Yews are not exactly drop dead gorgeous in July. They're boring then and even boringer in a box in January.

OK, if you have small conifers planted along the foundation, you need the protection because of the extra snow load sliding off the

roof. But I plant evergreens away from the house where I can see them—through the window of course—and they are expected to hold their own.

A graceful evergreen, branches laden with a few inches of snow, is a thing of beauty. By January standards at least. And yes, the occasional two foot snowfall has broken branches from time to time, but they grow back.

My favorite winter evergreens are in the chamaecyparis or false cypress family. For reasons I have never understood they are fairly uncommon.

At the end of the path that runs off the patio, but visible out my study window, is a chamaecyparis called 'Boulevard', an eighteen-foot beauty that was supposed to grow only to ten feet. But who cares. Visitors notice it from a distance because of its silver-edged blue foliage. Up close it is even better because the needles are soft, not prickly. Who would want a straggly pine when such ever-greens are available.

Closer to the window is one called 'Snow'. It has that name for its spring flush, when all the new growth turns pure white making the whole thing look like a scoop of vanilla ice cream. 'Snow' has been growing for over ten years and is only three feet tall. Wouldn't that look better in front of the house than the same yews that every neighbor has?

Chamis—pronounced kam-eez—as their aficionados call them, come in hundreds of varieties in every size, shape, and color from golden to blue to silver. If you want to plant a garden that will look great in winter, you won't go wrong with chamae-cyparis. And they look great in the warmer seasons, too.

If you love the look of blue spruce but don't have a place for one of the 80 foot giants, look for one called 'Montgomery'. Mine is about three feet high and four feet wide, and it has taken a decade to get there.

14

Most plants that are not evergreens are dead, or at least faking it. People who put burlap boxes around their yews are the same people who clear the brown perennial growth from their borders in fall. There is medication for this, though the side effects may adversely involve laundry and personal hygiene.

I leave the stubble for several reasons. For one, it gives texture and form to an otherwise flat white surface. It also leaves me something to do in March, when you really want to do something in the garden but it is too early to plant. For those who need a more functional excuse, it provides winter protection for the plants. Most don't need it, but somewhat tender plants like chrysanthemums are more likely to survive with their own self-made mulch.

One dead plant that even the most fastidious can live with is ornamental grass. Grasses are graceful in summer, even attractive in their way, but they come into their own in winter, providing a vertical element that is so often missing.

My favorite is 'Morning Light'. It grows to eight feet in the ground, maybe five feet in a tub on the patio where it makes a dramatic statement. But though it is rock hardy in the ground, it may need some help in a tub on the deck. No big problem. Just run a circle of chicken wire around the pot and fill it with leaves. This protection is not the prettiest sight out your window, but a few inches of snow will take care of that.

Another vertical element might be a garden statue or ornament. I would prefer something classic and elegant, but even those smarmy little garden gnomes are more interesting to look at than the tundra. If your birdbath or statue or gnome is in another part of the garden, it is worth the little effort it takes to move it. A minute's work, five months of a more interesting view.

Ornaments are made of different materials at varying prices, and both factors figure in whether you want to leave them outside in winter. Concrete is pretty tough, clay less so. I have both. Some I leave out to enhance my winter landscape. But if I paid any kind of serious money for it, I bring it in.

A little 12-volt spotlight on an ornament or evergreen adds even more interest, which brings us to another aspect of winter. Not only is it cold, it's dark. While in summer garden lights don't come on until 9:00 or so, in winter they are on when you come home from work. And from inside, garden lights turn a black window pane into a picture.

A few inches of snow brings out a special charm in garden lighting. If they are snow-covered, you don't see the fixture. All you see is a patch of glowing snow. Really pretty.

This points up a big flaw in solar lighting. With the weak sun and short days of winter, they don't collect enough energy for much of a show at night. And under a couple inches of snow, they collect none at all. No glowing snow. Often no light at all, at least not past dinner.

If you don't yet have garden lights, there is nothing like the early darkness of midwinter to inspire you. And it's something you can really do in the garden in January. You don't need warm weather and thawed soil to set them up. At least not the first time.

You can buy the components separately or get a kit with everything you need—a transformer, wire, and fixtures. Look for one that has both low path lights and at least one or two spots. Plug the transformer in and run the wire across the snow; the next snowfall will cover it up. Set the low fixtures where they will look nice out the window and the spots to highlight whatever plants or statues might be left. If you want, you can make a more permanant installation next spring, after you clear the stubble of last summer's perennials.

Winter installation shouldn't take more than half an hour. And doing it in January will focus your arrangement on the window. You won't end up with the typical summer display of mushroom lights along the front shrubs.

While you are setting the lights, you can be planning where you could put them in summer, which might be the best part of stringing lights in January. Any excuse to think of summer in January is welcome.

Junk

Companies must think gardeners are stupid. Maybe they're right. Or maybe they know that when gardeners are sitting in the dead of winter with a table full of catalogs, checkbook in hand and the fever upon them, they'll buy almost anything. At any price. How else to explain the pot tamper.

Who would pay $25.95 for a two and a half inch wooden pot tamper? It's a hunk of wood, fur cryin' out loud. Not a very big hunk of wood at that. The sort of thing left over and thrown away after any small project. Besides, knuckles work just fine for lightly tamping down soil.

The same catalog has a twenty-two dollar soil sieve. Twenty centimeters. I'm not sure how big twenty centimeters is, but I think it's pretty small.

A soil sieve is actually handy when making up potting soil or lightly covering a seed bed, but it should be a foot and a half or so wide, depending on how big a scrap of hardware cloth you can rummage up. Nail it to a square made of leftover lumber or that ugly picture frame in the attic. Total cost—let me add this up— uh, nothing.

Here is a "pro" seeder for $17.95. I guarantee that no pro has ever used it, but "professional" and its diminutives are good, if meaningless, marketing words. There are many kinds of seeders, some less expensive, some downright cheap. I know. I have them all. And none of them works as well as slicing off the top of the seed packet, making a crease in the middle of the front panel, and gently tapping the edge. Cost? Well, you already have a pair of scissors, don't you?

 There is a sunlight calculator for $26.95. It "measures the amount of sunlight in different areas of your garden." Here's a cost saving idea. LOOK UP! That's free.

Every catalog has some sort of raised bed brackets. Now, no one is a more enthusiastic proponent of raised beds than I am, but jeez. Here's a set for only seventy five bucks, and you supply the

lumber. How much do twelve wood screws cost? This is the argument for brackets: wood screws rot out. Mine last maybe ten years. So OK, how much do 24 wood screws cost? To be fair, factor in inflation.

You can find soil thermometers for as little as ten bucks. Soil thermometers are good. Experienced gardeners plant by soil temperatures rather than some arbitrary date on a calendar. Old timers say that you can transplant tomatoes when you can comfortably sit bare bottomed on the soil for three minutes. A thermometer is less likely to distress your neighbors. But you can get a decent thermometer for a dollar and change at the local megamart. It doesn't say "soil" on the package, but 70 degrees is 70 degrees. Just sink the tip four inches deep.

There are a few expensive items that are worth spending good money for. Felco pruners cost about fifty dollars—two pot tampers. They'll last a lifetime and your children will fight over them when the time comes. Maybe you will never have a Rolex or a Lexus, but you can have the very best pruners in the world.

For a little less than that you can get something I'll bet you never thought about—a heat mat. A heating mat provides bottom heat, the magical success component of propagation. Seeds will leap out of the cell pack and cuttings will root in a quarter of the time. With a heating mat and a fluorescent light fixture you can go into the nursery business, at least part time with a table in the front yard. Big name nurseries have started as modestly.

If you still have money and an itch to spend it, have I got a deal for you—a genuine reproduction of a Victorian (anything called Victorian sells) garden planning kit. Two pieces of paper and a pencil. Plus a special free bonus, a genuine wooden straight edge; just pay separate shipping and handling. Only $29.95 plus S&H. I'll take cash.

Remodel

January is resting time. Gardening season is over. Gardening season has not yet begun. It is a month of hot tea and books.

At least that's true in winters when I'm not putting in a new kitchen. For reasons beyond the ken of males, a perfectly functional kitchen which is less than half the age of this 1880 house was no longer acceptable to some who live here.

Plants have insinuated their way into the plans, though it has involved some minor subterfuge. I explained that swapping out an existing window for a slightly shorter greenhouse window would provide extra light and three feet more counter space. Counter space wins every argument.

And the sink base has been bumped out six inches so a half wall the height of the backsplash can create a tiled shelf, perfect for displaying fancy bottles of vinegars and oils. Perhaps later we will explore whether the sun from the window will degrade these delicate condiments, and perhaps the shelf might make a more hospitable home for some small plants.

Normal people go about a remodeling project thinking only of humans or sometimes their furry friends. Often, though, a little forethought and minor adjustments can make for a more plant friendly home.

Windowsills, for instance. Modern windows hardly have any. A bright window wasted. As long as you have all the molding off anyway, why not put in a wider sill? Even if you have no plant

plans at the moment, you might in the future, and it's a whole lot easier to do it now.

Skylights are popular in remodeling projects, but where do people put them? In the middle of the room, right? Do you have plants sitting in the middle of the room? OK, I do, but you probably don't. Or they put it directly over the shower—I know you don't have plants there.

What about putting the skylight in that dark back corner. You know, the one where the plants are anyway. Not only will it be good for the plants, it will be good for the room. When houses had two 15 amp circuits, every room had only one light, and it was in the middle of the ceiling. We don't do that any more because it's ugly and boring. Why do it with a skylight.

Maybe you're putting one of those new floating floor systems in the family room. They're beautiful, durable, and easy. But why not do a couple of feet in front of the sliding patio doors with ceramic tile. You can pretend it's a mud space, but it's really a place for large patio plants in winter. You won't have far to move them, and they'll just love the light.

If your plans for that room go beyond a new floor, you can think about lighting. Recessed spots above the tile strip will give the plants a little extra light as well as making a dramatic nighttime focal point, like drapes of light. Close your eyes and picture it.

The new kitchen will have a new floor and a new ceiling and almost everything in between, but one thing will remain, the ceiling hook over the kitchen sink. Though I might get a more decorative one. It is indispensable for tending and grooming hanging plants. I did make sure the new sink was large to accommodate the mess it can make.

Speaking of messes, our new plan doesn't have a mud room with a tile floor, but if it did, I'd want a floor drain in it. For washing out the mud, of course. And just in case I needed to hose off a mealy bug infested plant in winter.

Most cabinet books show at least one picture of a potting and plant care area, usually with a utility sink, usually absolutely gorgeous. That would be nice, but blatant, and I know the limitations of my persuasive powers.

January Thaw

Readers of a certain age will recall with nostalgia earlier years when they could go to bed at night and get up in the morning with no perambulations in between. We were confidant that the plumbing fixtures would sleep through the night as snugly as we did and found no need to get up in the wee hours to check.

Now we sleep in split shifts, but that is only a minor inconvenience, not a big problem. The same is true of our plants.

Just about every year we get a warm spell in the middle of winter. The plants sleeping outdoors stir and stretch and my phone starts to ring—nervous gardeners frantic about daffodils and crocus.

Hardy bulbs are used to this. There have always been winter warm spells of varying degrees and durations and the bulbs have adapted for millions of years. The first three or four calls, I tell them not to worry. After a while I get irritated and start telling callers they have to go out and push the sprouts back down into the ground.

This year's January thaw was a bit longer and a bit warmer than the common variety, but still within the norms. It is not—I repeat NOT—an indicator of global warming. Still there has been sprouting beyond what we usually see. And, I regret to say, there may be some consequences.

Many perennials got frisky during the week of fiftyish weather we had and started to grow. What they will look like in June depends on how much they grew.

A little sprouting at the base is inconsequential. They'll roll over, go back to sleep, and be fine when warm weather really comes. If they got a bit taller, there may be tip burn on the mature leaves. If that bothers you, trim the tips once the leaves get full sized.

21

If they really jumped up, the new growth may die back and be replaced by a more timely revivification. This strains the plants slightly, but it's nothing they can't cope with. Help them along with an early spring feeding.

Flowering trees and shrubs are more problematic. If the buds swelled enough and then got hit suddenly with very cold weather, you may lose this season's flowers. And on fruit trees, that means you may lose some of this year's fruit. You'll just have to wait until next year. Be thankful you don't earn your living as an orchardist.

I could lapse here into a philosophical homily about living with nature, accepting her blessings and enduring her whims. That's what I could do, but it's not my style. Instead I'll nag about what you should have done in the first place to prevent the problems.

For the most part it isn't warm air that causes plants to break dormancy. It's ground temperature. Though many gardeners don't understand this, winter mulch is intended to keep the ground cold, not warm. Cold ground keeps sprouts from sprouting and buds from budding.

Does that mean you should run out now and mulch? Well, maybe. If your ground is frozen, it wouldn't hurt to put some branches from the Christmas tree over the more tender perennials, especially shallow rooted ones like mums, to keep it frozen. But don't do it DURING a thaw or you'll make it worse.

Before long the soil will warm and stay warm, and before we know it flowers will be blooming. And if the January thaw has made them less than perfect, they will still be welcome enough.

Avocado

On occasion, when those little individual shrimp cocktails in the glass jars are marked down enough to suggest salmonella, my wife picks up a couple. We aren't worried, because these are essentially jars of cocktail sauce with scattered shrimp molecules, but there isn't enough seafood in them to support a toxic culture.

"Finding a shrimp in the cocktail sauce" could replace "finding a needle in a haystack" as an expression of a futile task, so we don't grab a fork and start rummaging around. Instead we pour one on a small block of cream cheese and spread it on crackers. Pretty good and pretty easy.

Some people clean those little glasses and put them in the cupboard, where they gradually migrate to the back and remain there until the kids come in to fight over the estate. No one fights over the shrimp glasses. But these things do have a use.

One of the fun projects of winter gardening is growing an avocado plant from the pit. The books tell you to stick toothpicks in the side to suspend the pit over a glass of water, but those little shrimp jars are perfect for the task, and you don't need toothpicks. The waist of the glass holds the pit at exactly the right height.

This is a wonderful project for a child or an adult with the horticultural acumen of a child. Just plop the pit in the jar and fill it with water so that the water just touches the bottom of the pit. The bottom is the part with the dimple. The top is rounded.

In many cases the pit will fit the jar like a cork, so the water doesn't evaporate. It's a good idea, though, to put it on the windowsill over the kitchen sink so you can watch and top off the water level should it drop below the bottom of the pit or change it if it gets yucky.

Eventually a thick white root will emerge from the bottom of the pit. I don't know how long it will take. It depends on the temperature of your house and the mood of the pit. It can be as soon as a couple of weeks or as long as a couple of months.

After the root has checked things out and determined it is safe, the pit will begin to split open and the top will start to grow. Now it is time for some actual gardening stuff.

Pot it up in a six-inch pot using good potting soil. Theoretically you can plant it with the top of the pit just below the surface, but  for people with watering issues it can be planted with the tip slightly exposed to avoid stem rot.

This is as easy as a transplanting job gets, and with any luck at all, your avocado should take off. It usually grows straight up. In three or four years it can develop into a single, straight stem with a tuft of leaves at the top tickling your ceiling.

Neophytes are perfectly happy with this, delighted in fact just that it lived. Most of us, though, would prefer something a little more shapely. That brings up the dreaded "P" word—pruning. Or pinching.

When the avocado gets about a foot high, cut off the top two inches, which includes most of the leaves. It will sprout from the sides. Honest, it will. When the side branches get long enough, cut the tips off those.

If this scares you, there is another way. Let the main stem grow to about 18 inches and bend it back toward the ground, making an inverted "U." Tie it to the main stem to keep it in place. Eventually this too will cause new sprouts to grow off the main stem, though it looks pretty silly while you're waiting.

Will you ever get an avocado off your tree? Probably not, but it could happen. But you'll get a decent, and cheap, house plant. And you will finally find a use for those little shrimp jars.

FEBRUARY

Plant History

Winter is a time for relaxing in an easy chair, reading perhaps, or just musing. This is a lofty activity that my wife sometimes mistakes for dozing. A cold, blizzardy Sunday in February is the perfect occasion to lock the kids out of the study, put the Goldberg Variations on the player, fire up a favored pipe, lean back, close your eyes, and ponder the larger picture, the higher plane. You guessed it. You'll get no useful information from me today. I am about to indulge myself in one of my rare but nonetheless dreaded contemplative spasms.

People sometimes ask why I'm so fascinated by plants. The tone of voice clearly implies that I'm wasting my time and the subject is too trivial for even my slim talents. No one seems aware that plants play an indispensable role in the history of earth, of life, of us.

For example, the single most important invention since Creation was made about three and a half billion years ago by a blue-green alga, a single-celled plant so primitive that it didn't even have a digital watch or a wrist to wear it on. Like many seminal inventors, we don't know his name. This plant learned to take water and carbon dioxide, and using sunlight for energy (an idea we're still fiddling with), make simple sugar and free oxygen. Without this process we would have neither food to eat nor air to breathe.

Think back to tenth grade botany. There may be the mist of a memory of photosynthesis; perhaps the word chlorophyll meanders across the mind, the stuff of toothpaste and air freshener ads in the fifties. But no one impressed on us then how utterly essential it all was.

The sugar made by photosynthesis is the base line of the food chain. Plants use this sugar to make more complex carbohydrates,

proteins, and fats. Animals eat the plants or eat the animals that eat the plants and produce other proteins and fats. Ultimately that beautifully marbled T-bone on your plate started out as pond slime. *Bon appétit.*

Pure oxygen, a byproduct of this natural manufacturing process, was released into a primeval atmosphere of carbon dioxide, methane, and ammonia. (Oxygen was considered a pollutant by activist algae, but they had not yet evolved hands to carry picket signs.) To prepare the world for animal life, tiny plants worked for eons pumping out oxygen.

Eventually complex plants, then animals evolved and got along without us quite well, thank you, for a few billion years. Over the eons forests covered the land, then receded, surrendering some of the land to grasses. As the forest shrank, so did the habitat of ancient forest-dwelling apes. One species was evicted from its primordial home to live or die on the new savanna. Some say he had to rear up on his hind legs to watch for danger in the high grass, and hands designed to grasp branches were free to pick up a rock, later to shape it. Others contend that this ape was already bipedal, which is what allowed him to move to grassland. Whichever the case, apes that remained in the forest remained apes. The savanna biped took off on an important evolutionary journey, and the change in vegetation was his ticket.

Just when that hominid became human is hotly disputed. It is clear, though, that when Homo began to think, it was fully *Homo sapiens.* Bones and crude stone tools cannot tell us when that happened. But one spring day 60,000 years ago a Neanderthal in Iraq laid a dead comrade in the back of a cave. When archaeologists excavated, dense clusters of microscopic pollen grains were found, the first evidence that our ancestors thought not just of the next meal, but also of the next life. Primitive man had become a sentient human being, and the rite of passage was marked by a bouquet of bachelor buttons.

Though the rudiments of abstract thought had begun, man was hardly civilized. Over the next fifty millennia humans remained hunter-gatherers, small groups following their food. Then 10,000 years ago, not far from where the Neanderthal lay buried with flowers, our ancestors had another vital encounter with plants.

Today, after decades of intensive work by plant breeders, a few tetraploid hybrids have made it into our gardens. These plants are the harbinger of a revolution in horticulture. They have doubled their normal number of chromosomes, which causes them to perform extravagantly, but they are difficult to produce and are seldom fertile. It is hard to imagine that such focused hybrids could occur naturally, but they did.

Stone age people had long eaten the small, scant seed of wild wheat, similar to the foxtail grass that grows along fences, but the seed head was too small to be a major source of food. Then this wild wheat crossed accidentally with another wild grass to create tetraploid emmer wheat. It was larger, more vigorous, and —incredibly—it was fertile. It could be cultivated. And then it did it again! The second natural hybrid was bread wheat, with even more chromosomes, and it was fertile, too!

This accidental development of grass into a plant with agricultural potential was the beginning of the Neolithic Revolution. A population could feed itself with abundance; cities became possible, even inevitable. And though some may wish to deny it, both culturally and etymologically cities *are* civilization. Hundreds, then thousands of people, some freed from the labor of food production to pursue more elevated ventures, could live together in permanent settlements, forming a critical mass where ideas and innovations proliferated. After a million years of savagery, in a geological eyeblink we were walking on the moon. All because of an improbable crossing between wild grasses.

The next ten thousand years include most of those events that are commonly listed as milestones. Most were simply advances in agriculture that allowed the advancement of empires that did it or compelled the conquest of those who had it.

Modern history begins with the Age of Discovery in the 15th Century, and plants figure prominently. In the span of one lifetime

Europeans increased the size of their world tenfold. Why? They were looking for plants. Diaz rounded Africa, deGamma sailed to India, and Columbus discovered the New World, all in a search for spices. Plants.

The invention of paper from plants made possible the invention of printing, and knowledge was finally available to all. Early development of medicines from plants, like quinine and penicillin, doubled our life spans.

Today plants in some way provide the livelihood for most of the world's population. They make our food and our air, as well as provide the raw materials to make medicines, clothes, and houses. Plant material heats our homes and generates our power. Almost incidentally they give us great beauty.

These crucial contributions to our lives will never be given their due, of course. No national plant history month. There are no leafy lobbyists, no PR plants. But now you know, and you might think of this larger picture the next time you grudgingly pull a weed or water your fern. The next time you smell a lilac.

There. I feel better. The snow has stopped, so has the music, and the kids are pounding on the door. I think I'll go water my house plants. And maybe say thank you under my breath.

Sun

It's a sure sign of impending spring: About nine thirty the morning sun glares off the screen of the small television by my computer. That's OK; there's not much worth watching at 9:30—I just listen to Washington Journal—and the problem will go away by 10:30, and it will be gone completely by March.

Soon that spring sun will find the fish tank and the water will turn green. All winter the pump and filter have kept up, but as the sun creeps north and hits the sheltered window, it makes just too good an environment for the algae, and they flourish. After a couple of weeks the sun will move on and the water will clear.

People who don't garden think the sun rises in the east and sets in the west. Gardeners know better. Or they should. A good gardener needs to be an astronomer.

I'll tell you why in a minute. But first let's look at the basics.

The sun rises in the east and sets in the west on only two days a year, the summer and winter equinox. The rest of the year it rises and sets either north or south of that axis. So in summer the sun rises in the northeast and sets in the northwest. Face north and hold your arms out as if you are going to hug someone. You are roughly pointing to the sunrise and sunset in June. Turn around and you have the December parameters, southeast and southwest.

In addition to moving around the horizon, it changes its arc. In winter it stays low in the sky, even at noon, which is why it can duck under the porch roof and hit my fish tank. In summer it shines straight down from high overhead.

Take a flashlight and shine it straight down on a piece of paper. It makes a circle, right? Now shine it at an angle. The circle is now an oval, or a parabola or something, covering maybe three times

more of the paper surface. Same amount of light, spread out more, so any point gets weaker light than when you shine straight down. That's why my sun-shy begonias can take a sunny window in winter and thrive, but noon sun outside in summer would kill them.

That is why you so often see instructions on some annuals and perennials to avoid midday sun, but the spread-out morning or evening sun, when it is making a parabola, are fine. If you plant impatiens where they get sun in early afternoon, they'll wilt, then perk back up in the evening.

Because the sun moves, you can't go out on any particular day and identify the sunniest and shadiest spots in your garden. It might be fine for that day, but three months down the road the conditions could be different.

Let's say you go out on a nice day in March to plan your garden for the season. There's an area next to the house under the eaves or under a tree that is bathed in sun, great for sun loving annuals like petunias or marigolds. But the sun is still pretty low in March, and as it gets higher in the sky, those eaves and trees will block light for much of the day. The plants will still grow, but they won't flower like the pictures in the magazines.

Or lets say you decide to plant some impatiens in the open shade cast by a hedge, that perfect early light and mid-day protection we talked about. But as the sun gets higher in the sky, the shadow shrinks. What was in shade in March can be devastated by the sun by July.

So you can't go out one day in March to see where the sun shines. You must go out into your garden every day and look around. Which is a pretty good way for a gardener to spend time.

Onions

Gentlemen, START YOUR ONIONS.

How's that for a lead! Images of the big Memorial Day race, the beginning of summer, just the thing we need here, now, in the dregs of winter. When seeds start growing on the windowsill, can summer be far away? Well, it can, but onion seeds need that time.

If you grow onions from sets, as most gardeners do, you can wait a few more weeks. Sets are immature onions grown from seed the year before and stored over the winter. Of necessity onions grown from sets must be storage type onions, so that the sets will keep through the winter to plant again.

30

 About the time onion sets are piling up in garden centers, Vidalia onions arrive in grocery stores. Grown through the winter in Georgia (in Vidalia county, would you believe?), they are mild and sinfully sweet. When they are in season, potato salad and chopped liver are nothing but a medium for chopped Vidalia onions. A hamburger topped with a slab is, well, there aren't words.

Enjoy your Vidalias while you can, though, because by July they'll be gone. If you bought enough to last a while, you'll find them rotted in the basement. They don't keep. There can be no Vidalia onion sets.

Some Northern gardeners try to grow "Vidalias" from seed. The real name of the variety is Granex, and you'll see it in catalogs and find it in racks. But the onions you'll grow here are a pitiful imitation of the real thing. We're in the wrong latitude.

Here we need onions that are planted in spring and bulb up in summer. 'Ailsa Craig' and 'Kelsae Sweet Giant' are two large and sweet onions developed in England for Northerners.

Whatever seed you try, this is the time to start. Have you always failed with seeds indoors? Don't worry about it. Onions are dead easy. Even people who screw up marigolds can start onions from seed, and it doesn't take any fancy equipment..

Start with a flat. Cottage cheese tubs are good for maybe 20 seedlings, a microwave cake pan for 50. Punch half a dozen holes in the bottom and fill it with seed starting mix, usually on sale in March. This stuff is packed dry and is maddeningly difficult to moisten. Open the bag and pour in a couple cups of warm water, knead the bag like a sore shoulder, pour in some more, and knead some more, until it's slightly damp.

Onion seed is good sized and easy to handle. Scatter it on the surface so you have something like four seeds per square inch. That's just a guide; don't get neurotic about it. If I see you get a ruler out, I'll slap your wrist. Dust the surface with dry potting mix. It's paler

than the moistened soil; use just enough to make the surface the lighter color. Then seal the flat in a bread bag.

Ignore all that stuff you've heard about bottom heat. Keep the containers at room temperature and the onions will be up and growing in days.

Also ignore my advice not to grow seedlings on a windowsill. Once the onion seeds are up, take the bag off and put them on a windowsill. They'll look awful, simply dreadful, but they'll make it. When they get spindly and fall over, take scissors and chop them back to four inches; it's just like mowing the lawn. Feed them with liquid fertilizer at quarter strength once a week if you think of it. Whatever you do, short of total and endless drought, they'll survive.

In late April, earlier if you're gutsy, take them to the garden and knock them out of the flat. You'll find a tangle of roots. Tease them apart and crudely poke them into the fertilized ground. Mulch them with spring grass clippings to keep moisture in and weeds out. Fertilize monthly and water during dry spells. And get ready to amaze your neighbors.

It's that simple. They're foolproof. Almost. You know how you learned Dick and Jane before Shakespeare? Onions are a primer for seed starting. You'll learn procedures, gain confidence, and you can eat your lessons.

With that success under your belt, you should be pumped up to try other seeds, not as idiot-proof as onions, but still easy.

Starting flower and vegetable seeds indoors makes great good sense for many reasons. You can save a few bucks, but that is minor (a difficult confession for a Scot). I grow my own to get a wider choice. While nurseries may offer a dozen kinds of tomato, seed catalogs have hundreds. 'SunGold' cherry tomato is reason in itself to learn seed starting. And varieties sold in nurseries are bred to have qualities that help them sell, like early blooming. and garden performance is secondary. Try a pack of 'Inca' marigolds from the nursery and some 'First Lady' marigolds that you grow yourself and decide which you like better in July. Still another reason is to get the hundreds of flowers you want instead of the dozen you can afford in May.

Most seeds don't need planting as early as onions. Start peppers and petunias in the middle of March, tomatoes a week or two later, marigolds a week after that. There are charts showing the appropriate timing for common plants in many garden books and spring magazines. Check them out while you're waiting to pay for the groceries.

Plant your seeds in trays and bread bags just like the onions. You can put them on the kitchen table and they'll be up and growing in a week or two. Or you can speed it up with a little extra heat. You'll find warm spots on top of TV set, refrigerator, and water heater. (Did you ever wonder why they call them hot water heaters when they are actually cold water heaters?)

As soon as green shows, they'll need all the light they can get. Anyone who actually took my advice and built a fluorescent light stand (see page 36) has got it made. Otherwise you need to go with your sunniest windowsill. To make the most of it, cut a piece of corrugated cardboard from the largest box you can find, cover it with aluminum foil, and prop it up behind the seed flats. Just how you prop it up depends on your particular windowsill, but the contrivance usually involves duct tape.

 Once the seedlings have three or four true leaves and begin to crowd, we come to the tricky part. You must separate them and pot them up into plastic six packs—you know, the ones piled out in the garage from springs past. You did save them, didn't you?

Wash them off, fill with the same kind of dampened potting mix you started the seeds in, spread some newspapers on the counter, grab a spoon, and hold your breath. With the spoon, dig out a small section of soil with a few seedlings. Make a hole in each section of the six pack with the spoon handle or some equivalent weapon, carefully tease out single seedlings from the clump, hold them by

33

the leaves, and plop them into the holes. Water them in carefully; a turkey baster works well for this job.

It is a nerve-wracking job the first time you do it, and though it does take composure and care, it isn't as touchy as I make it sound. By next year you'll be doing it without shaking. Back into the light, tape the foil back up, feed lightly, and voilà, you're a real gardener. That's a good reason to start your own seeds.

But the best reason is that you don't have to wait another two months to start gardening.

Brassicas

I don't like to write about cole crops. My spell checker insists they don't exist, and being orthographically challenged, I'm afraid to argue with it. So I'll try to break an old habit and start calling them brassicas instead. It's an extra syllable, but it saves me from the exasperation of that constant, accusatory beeping.

The brassicas are a family that's been in the news almost as much as celebrity breakups. I won't quote all of the study results, because they'll probably change next week, but in a nutshell, brassicas are good for you. And they're easy to grow. Mostly.

These cole crops—DARN! There it goes again—these brassicas are only a part of the crucifer family, though. Crucifers include radishes, turnips, cress, kale, horseradish, nasturtiums, and even woad, should you ever get the urge to dye your body blue and fight the Romans. But the cole crops—DAMN!—are specifically the cabbages.

You may be surprised to learn that broccoli, cauliflower, Brussels sprouts, and cabbage are all really the same plant, *Brassica oleracea*. The primitive cabbage made those changes in the Middle Ages, mostly by itself, sometimes with a little help, changing from an open, leafy plant to a tight head. In another medieval farmer's field another one grew a long stalk with little cabbages sprouting from it. Another formed a large flower bud at the top, yet another a tight fleshy bud near the ground.

Noting this, primitive farmers collected seed from these strange plants and sowed it. Most reverted to the original form, but a few kept the new genetic characteristics. Over generations seed was produced that always grew into the mutant form. This is called selection, and from selection we got cabbage, Brussels sprouts, broccoli, and cauliflower, all genetically engineered by nature.

Being pretty much the same plant, they need pretty much the same treatment, which pretty much everybody gets wrong. If you go to the nursery in May and buy broccoli and tomato transplants to put out Memorial Day weekend, you're one of them. Broccoli may be the same as cauliflower, but it is very different from tomatoes.

Tomatoes thrive in heat, but the col... (Hah! Caught myself.) the brassicas like it cool, even frosty. They can and should be planted out before the last average frost date in weather that would turn a tomato into blackened mush.

Most garden centers haven't caught on to this yet, or they think you haven't, so you've got to start your own seeds to have them ready at the right time. And the time to start them is soon.

It's no problem. Fill some of last year's left over cell packs with seed starting mix, sprinkle two or three seeds into each cell, and cover with just enough soil so they are no longer visible. Don't forget to label them, because they all look alike as seedlings. Once up, nip off all but the strongest seedling in each cell and put them on a south facing windowsill. For best use of the light, put a large piece of aluminum foil taped to some cardboard behind them.

Plant them outside in mid to late April into soil that has been turned and well fertilized. And though water is seldom a problem in April, make sure the soil remains moist. These plants grow fast, so don't want to slow them down with inadequate food and water.

Most of the brassicas are fast crops and will mature in early summer. It will give you something to eat while you're waiting endlessly for the tomatoes to ripen.

Once you have eaten them all, you have that bare garden space, so start all over again. In mid July you can plant seeds directly into the garden for plants that will mature in the cool days of fall.

An exception to this drill is Brussels sprouts, which take their good old time, from 90 to 120 days depending on conditions and variety. Also they taste best after they've been exposed to several hard fall frosts, so you don't even want to think about harvest until October. My Brussels sprouts are direct seeded into the garden in early summer.

If you wait to plant the brassicas to mature during the heat of summer, you will get tasteless, sometimes bitter crops. And more important, you'll sit inside just dreaming of fresh food for weeks while the rest of us are outside gardening.

Free February Resolutions

Last month I resolved not to make any more New Year's resolutions. So far I haven't broken it. How are you doing with yours? But the itch is still there, so I'll make resolutions for other people. For free. Here's one to add to your list.

BE IT RESOLVED that this year I (that means you) shall finally set up that light garden I've been thinking about for lo these many seasons. Then I can start dozens of seedlings, and Campbell will stop nagging me.

For those who have not heard this tirade before, we'll sing the old song one more time. Regular readers can join in on the chorus.

You don't need one of those costly units in the catalogs. A twelve dollar shop light—48 inches, two tubes—hung from the joists in the basement will let you to start up to sixteen dozen seedlings. At a buck and a half a six pack, that's forty eight dollars worth of plants. Even taking into account the cost of seeds, soil, and trays and cell packs (if you're too profligate to save them and pile them in the garage like the rest of us) you come out ahead the very first year. Your light garden is free, and next year it's even freer.

I've suggested setting your fixture up in the basement. Mine actually sits next to a foundation window where it glows eighteen hours a day. No one has ever called the police. Either they think I am too upstanding to grow anything illegal, or maybe just too manifestly uncool.

The books always say to adjust the height so that the tubes are no more than two inches above the tops of the plants. I swear the people who write this stuff have never actually grown a plant. The plants under your lights don't all grow to the same height at the same rate.

Better is to set the lights so they accommodate your tallest plant and prop the shorter ones up. Inverted flower pots work for individual plants. For large seed flats, those big slabs of Styrofoam from the appliance box you threw out would have worked great. You'll find something.

If your basement is very warm, though, that might not be the best spot. Seedlings grow weak and spindly in warm temperatures. Low sixties during the day, cooler at night is what you're looking for. Maybe an unused bedroom would be better than a cellar next to the furnace.

Astute gardeners may grumble that, sure, seedlings like cool temperatures, but they need warmth to germinate. True, but they don't need much light then. The ballast in the fixture gives off heat, so put newly planted flats in a bread bag and set them on TOP of the fixture until the first sprouts show, then move them down under the light. I could try to talk you into a heat mat, but one step at a time.

Of course you don't want an ugly shop light hanging in a bedroom. So tart it up. Spend an extra two dollars for a can of spray paint to match the wallpaper and use brass decor hooks in the ceiling. You could even glue a little lace along the edge of the light; that's what my wife would do.

If space is an issue, here's another idea—a few more dollars, but still within the first year payback. Buy a 2- by 4-foot piece of half inch plywood, four 12-inch coffee table legs, and some contact paper, something pretty. Cover the plywood with contact paper, attach the legs, and bolt the fixture to the underside. The job is so easy you can do it yourself; you don't need to ask your husband and then wait until July.

This eliminates the chains and hooks, and whatever was on the floor you can pile on top. Better still, you can put another light garden on top, double decked, and you still have the same space to pile stuff. In the off season, unscrew the legs and shove the whole thing under the bed with the dust covered exercise machine.

The fixture probably comes without tubes. You don't need to buy the very expensive grow light tubes, and you don't want the very cheap shop light tubes. You want one standard 40 watt fluorescent tube, which used to be called cool white, and one slightly more expensive Kitchen and Bath tube, which used to be called warm white. This combination works about as well as those very expensive bulbs.

They often come in two-packs, but you really don't waste any money, because now you have a replacement set to change to next year. The bulbs should be changed each spring, even if they haven't burned out.

If everyone does this right now, I promise never to mention it again. But don't dawdle. In a couple of weeks we'll be starting the first seeds.

MARCH

Aftercare

Are you having an Agnes Gooch moment?

Auntie Mame said that all of life's a banquet, and most poor suckers are starving to death. Agnes Gooch took this to heart and later lamented, "I've lived, I've lived. But what am I going to do now?"

That's the attitude of many who welcomed blooming holiday and gift plants which now linger as dowdy green leaves. If that. Those potted tulips, for instance.

There is controversy about whether you can plant forced spring bulbs outside when the blooms fade. The answer is, Of course you can. Whether they will ever bloom again is a different question.

Daffodils and crocus have the best chance to recover and prosper. Take them out right now (if it isn't snowing) and plant them in the ground a little deeper than they were in the pot. Water them in with some liquid fertilizer.

The leaves will die back. They may be starting to already. No problem. In a few weeks you can plant some petunias right on top of them.

Tulips are more problematic. Unless you have very good soil and site, they probably won't do much. On the other hand, if you put them out on garbage day they won't do anything, so it is worth the chance. With all these bulbs, though, if you try to keep them in the pot with a hope of them blooming next spring, forget it.

The amaryllis can be left in its pot. Probably should be, though some people plant them in the open garden and pot them up again in fall.

While the spring bulbs can go outside now and forgotten, the amaryllis must be coddled a bit longer. The leaves should be growing now, so give them a sunny window and a drink of liquid fertilizer.

After the danger of frost is behind us, put the pot outside. An east exposure with some protection from midday sun is best, but they'll take what you give them. The more leaves, the bigger the bulb in fall, so feed it regularly. When fall arrives, throw the plant in the basement, stop watering, and let the leaves die back. DO NOT cut off green leaves; let them wither until they come off with a slight tug. Next winter it should bloom again.

Newly purchased Easter lilies are blooming now, filling the house with a scent you have to hack through with a machete to get to the kitchen. You can plant them outside in May. Next year they'll bloom in your garden, but they'll be taller and later.

About the time the lily fades, mothers will be wallowing in azaleas and hydrangeas and mums. Can they be planted out in the garden? I have no idea. Probably not.

Though there are hardy varieties of all of these, the Mothers Day plants are often bred for greenhouse culture and won't take our winters. Or maybe they will. But there is usually no way of knowing.

Here's how to find out if they're hardy. Plant them outside. If they are still alive next summer, they are.

The hydrangea, planted outside, probably won't die, but it may never bloom. Then you'll call me and ask why your hydrangea doesn't have any flowers, and frankly, I don't need any more of those calls. I'm thinking of putting the explanation on my answering machine.

The problem with florists' hydrangeas is that the shrub might be hardy but the flower buds aren't. They start to swell, get nipped by spring frost, and die.

Here's what you can do. Put the pot outside for the summer, water and feed it, then let it catch the first couple of frosts. Put it in a cold but not quite freezing spot, like an attached garage or an unheated sun porch or mud room. In February it will try putting out new leaves, and you can move it into warmer temperatures and bright light. It should bloom for you again. You can do the same thing with the azalea.

And then there is that garish red thing still sitting in the corner collecting dust, the Christmas poinsettia. Leave it there. With luck you will forget it and it will die. Then you won't be tempted to try reblooming it next winter.

Garden Prep

Increasingly spring looks like a sure thing instead of a distant hope. And with the first mild days comes one of the most pleasurable jobs of spring, the fall clean-up.

Looking at the shambles outside in its totality is daunting. Bushels of leaves loll around, scraps of paper have blown in, plant debris molders, pruning chores mock me, and everywhere is the unmistakable evidence that dogs live in this neighborhood. All conspire to dampen my resolve, to send me back inside for a cup of tea and one last romp through the seed catalogs.

 The solution is to break up one big job into several small, less intimidating jobs. So in March I have at my garden a few square feet at a time. It breaks the news to my winter withered muscles gently.

Small jobs need small tools, the handiest of which is a miniature lawn rake. But they're hard to find. That is, they're hard to find in stores, and they're hard to find in my March garden under the debris. Fall clean-up stalled once again.

41

Imagine my surprise to find exactly what I needed at the local Kmart, and for under three bucks. That's a third the price for the same sort of thing in an upscale garden store. The Kmart three dollar shrub rake just needs a bit of modification. Since my foot-by-foot cleanup is done mostly on my knees, I need a rake with a short handle, about a foot long. No problem. Half a minute with a saw and I have my short handled rake plus the severed end to put in the garage in case I ever need half a rake handle.

Don't laugh. Years ago at a yard sale I picked up the severed head of a great iron garden rake for 25 cents. Fitted with half a handle from my magic garage, it's perfect for working in the raised beds of the vegetable garden and the cramped quarters of the perennial bed. Which is where I've just been.

I go foot by foot, and each plant gets attention. This is the greatest joy of the earliest season, getting into the bedraggled perennial bed and making it orderly, a task the misguided did months ago. Last season's dead foliage is removed, bright new growth is exposed. Clumps that have grown too large are divided, the extras potted up. They can be planted later in another spot or given to friends or put out at the annual neighborhood yard sale.

With last season disposed of, the new season is launched. Each plant gets a helping of compost and some 5-10-5 fertilizer to get it off to a good start. How much? The granules on the ground should look like stars on a clear summer night. I scratch it into the surface of the soil.

Stakes and cages are put in position now, at least in theory, so the plant can grow up through them. Fresh mulch is added to the layer already there. Each year some of it breaks down and enriches the soil, so it must be periodically replenished.

 Raking the garbage out of the base of a clematis, I see that it is already well budded out. I have several clematis, and though this is bona fide spring work, not fall cleanup, it is work that will not wait.

There has been an inordinate amount of claptrap written about pruning clematis, some of it by me. There are three different types of clematis, and each has its own complicated pruning regimen. I have tried to explain it all to my readers, without success. I have tried to explain it to myself, also without success. In years past I have assiduously marked each plant according to type and gone into the garden with pruners in one hand and a book on clematis in the other.

Eventually I pruned down a dozen pages of incomprehensible instruction into one simple rule: cut off the dead stuff. This time of year that means anything that doesn't have big, fat buds. Stems that have puny buds should be trimmed back to a pair of big ones. Once the rats' nest of dead twigs is teased out, I sprinkle some of fertilizer and spread some mulch. Three square feet more of garden done. Move on.

As I muddle through the beds, occasional errant branches of shrubs and trees, grown long last summer, poke me in unexpected places. Pruning shears are always on my belt, and I clip them off. Some people call this pruning and get scared, but I call it just getting things out of the way.

 That should be enough for the first excursion, but on my way back to the house I see tulips coming up. And daffodils and crocus and some things I'm not sure what they are. They look hungry.

Spring blooming bulbs want to be fed just after they break ground. They'll muddle through for a few seasons with no care, but with an early spring feeding they will be bigger and better next year.

The very best bulb food, you will not be surprised to learn, is bulb food, the stuff sold in small boxes at a premium price made specifically for bulbs. But a close second, and a whole lot cheaper, is ordinary 5-10-5 garden fertilizer. That's what I use unless I happen to find a battered package of bulb food in the half-price bin.

43

The worst bulb food is bone meal, our grandmothers' favorite. It was fine in the olden days when it was ground up with yucky stuff still clinging to it. But now it is steamed and sterilized and has no nitrogen, which bulbs need. If you have a supply of bone meal, use it in the bottom of the planting hole for perennials and put 5-10-5 on your bulbs.

Some of the bulbs are pushing their way up through bright green ground cover that wasn't there last fall. Weeds. And these mat-forming weeds will take over by May if not removed now. Look and you will see they are already blooming, eager to spread enough seed to conquer the world, or at least your part of it.

Most mats grow from a central root. Slip your hand, with your thumb and index finger opened into a half circle, under the edges of the mat until you find the point where it attaches to the ground.

Pull.

After a winter of dangerous thinking, there are a couple of shrubs I need to move, one because I don't like where I put it, another because IT doesn't like where I put it. After five years it's half the size it would be if it were happy. This is the time of year to do it. I might as well do it while I'm out.

I prune back the tops by half and dig up as big a root ball as I can manage. I like to put them in pots for a few days and move them around to make sure I have the spot right. Even then sometimes I blow it, but they can always be moved again some future March.

Doing this work a few feet at a time will keep me busy through the month, working on good days, taking on more as my muscles wake up, probably waylaid briefly by at least one snowstorm. The first section I do is that part framed by the window next to chair, of course. Now it's time to sit down and appreciate the small job I got done.

Shade

Show me a gardener who has good soil in full sun and I will show you a gardener who longs for the problems that plague the rest of us. He'll complain that he has no shady spots or no boggy spots or no droughty spots, conditions demanded for some plants he wants to grow but can't. He is damned with a perfect gardening site.

There is an old saying that goes, "I cried because I had no sun, until I met a man who had no shade." Something like that. The truth is that shade can be a blessing, not a curse. Shade gardens are cool, calming, even lush. If you do it right.

First we have to talk about just what shade is. It is not darkness. Crawl under a pine tree and what do you find growing there? Nothing, not even weeds. If weeds won't grow there, don't try planting impatiens.

Shade is also not a spot that gets half a day's sunshine. Unfortunately such a spot is also not "full sun" though many people treat it that way. Sun loving plants in those circumstances will grow, even bloom, but they will never look like the catalog pictures. Many "shade tolerant" plants will grow and prosper if there is sufficient water.

Deep shade is the shade of the forest floor with a heavy canopy of trees but clear enough underneath to walk. There are plants that grow there, but you must do your homework and select carefully. One fine choice for a copse of leafy trees is naturalized daffodils. While these bulbs need sun, they bloom and ripen before the trees leaf out, so they get the sun when they need it.

A single deciduous tree or two gives you more light and more options. This is often called dappled shade. Light comes in around the edges and filters through the leaves.

The growing conditions under a yard tree can be improved by limbing up and thinning out. Limbing up a tree involves removing the lower branches so that sun can get in around the edges in the morning and evening. Thinning is the removal of some of the

45

upper branches, no job for an amateur, so that more light comes through the canopy.

The very best situation is called open shade, which you will find on the north side of a large building, like your house. In open shade the sun is blocked in the middle of the day, when it is most vicious, but the area is exposed to the whole sky. It is bright, but not sunny.

In fact open shade often does get some direct sun, but in the kindest way. A northern exposure will let the sun peek in in the early morning and late afternoon during the summer, giving plants there the most gentle of direct rays.

The best part, though, is that this does not happen in winter as the sun moves south with the retirees. Contrary to conventional wisdom, the sun is unwanted in winter. Not by us, but by plants. It causes leaves to transpire when the roots cannot replace the water from frozen soil. But when the sun travels south, it no longer peeks around the corner of a north facing garden.

A shade garden needs not only the right light but also the right soil. Most plants that grow in shade are woodland plants, and they like a woodland soil, moisture retentive yet open and airy with lots of organic matter. Dig in leaves, shredded bark, sawdust, even peat moss (one of the few places I allow peat moss). How much? Don't ask. Just keep digging.

When you have the right light and the right soil, you need the right plants.

I once had a neighbor who aspired briefly to be a gardener. She bought a six pack of marigolds and a six pack of impatiens and proceeded to plant the former on the north side of her house and the latter on the south. The impatiens burned out by July and the marigolds refused to bloom. She decided she didn't have a green thumb. In fact what she didn't have was a brain.

So you have a great shade gardening site, open shade on the north side of the house or dappled shade under a few trees, with moisture retentive, humusy soil and maybe a hint of sun in the morning and the evening. Don't blow it by planting petunias, no matter how much you like petunias. It should go without saying that you need shade loving plants, but in my experience nothing, no matter how obvious, can go without saying.

For the shoulders of the shade garden—-woody shrubs—rhododendrons (NOT rhododendrums, pul-LEASE) and azaleas are the norm. They are all rhododendrons, actually, but some have chosen to call themselves azaleas for reasons of their own, perhaps a—ahem—shady past. I know I won't talk you out of rhododendrons, but there are other choices.

Pieris (or andromeda, a common name perversely twice as long as the botanical) is an underused shrub. An evergreen, the new spring growth is bright red, accompanied by fountains of white flowers.

While pieris turns to fire in the spring, fothergilla blazes in the autumn with some of the brightest fall colors in the plant kingdom. Spring brings white flower with the unmistakable scent of honey. A variety called 'Blue Mist' is hot right now, but you need illegal drugs to see the blue, and the common species has much better fall color.

Mountain laurel is another welcome addition to the home garden. Even if they lose most of their leaves, older specimens acquire a stark architectural form, dramatic against the winter snow.

Once the shrubs are planted, it is time to choose perennials, and there are many. Hosta is the workhorse of shade perennials, with all the charm of that daunting draft animal. You have to have hosta in a shade garden—it's a rule—but leave room for more interesting plants.

Pulmonaria is one of my favorites for shade. The leaves, dappled with white or silver, brighten the spot, and the flowers in pink or white are a bonus.

Hellebores are thought to be a connoisseur's plant, but in the right spot they are vigorous growers. They are particularly treasured for their very early blooms, usually March, but February is not unknown.

Bergenia has stout flowers in June, and the foliage, often bronze, persists through the winter. Astilbe can bring a strong red or pink into the garden. And for the brightest white you've ever seen outside a soap commercial, plant some *Phlox divaricata* 'Fuller's White'.

A special treasure is the hardy cyclamen. Smaller than the florists cyclamen, the miniature flowers are nonetheless more than welcome in November, and the beautiful silvery leaves remain all winter long.

For the most part shade plants are quiet, calm, cool. But for pizzazz there is always impatiens. The New Guinea impatiens need a fair amount of sun, but the old busy Lizzie will paint the shade in dozens of colors. Or tuberous begonias, a shade flower that will put the most flagrant sun lover to shame.

If you do not have the rich organic soil that woodland plants prefer, if you have, say, concrete or soil resembling concrete, there are pots. With containers you can bring your garden up onto a porch, which is usually shaded pretty heavily by a roof.

There are hundreds, if not thousands of other plants for various degrees of shade. Don't overlook ferns and wildflowers. The point is that you don't have to bewail your lack of sun. Just choose more wisely than my neighbor and start planting.

Veg Bed

There are people who still believe that a vegetable garden must be out back and must consist of only vegetables. These are often people with fond childhood memories of long hours under a hot sun with a hoe. Character building, their fathers said. As adults,

 these people would rather eat soggy string beans out of cans for the rest of their lives than make a vegetable garden.

Well, you can do it. And you can do it without a hoe. In fact without much effort. Except once, the first year, at the beginning.

I have preached this sermon before, I know, and a few have come up to the altar. But you still sit there in your pew, unconvinced, so I am going to try one more time.

You need a four foot by eight foot deeply dug raised bed, and March is a fine time to get it started. Once the snow melts. And the ground dries, at least a little.

The frame is simple. You'll need three eight-foot 2 by 8's, one cut in half. I like pressure treated wood, but I know some have objections to it. It has been years since they stopped using arsenic in the treatment, and even then it was harmless to growing vegetables. But these prejudices hang on even when circumstances change.

You can use untreated wood, and it will last several years. If you have an opened can of the paint you used the last time you painted the house, slather some of that on and it will last even longer. The construction itself is about as simple as construction gets. Form the four pieces into a rectangle and put three three-inch screws into each joint.

That's the easy part. The next part is either very hard, or very very hard, depending on how well you want to do it. Naturally I suggest the second option, since I'm not the one doing it.

Take a good look at the ground where you are going to put the frame. A good look, because you will never see it again.

Since you will never see it again, it stands to reason that you will never again get a chance to work the soil and improve the soil. And the secret to growing a lot of vegetables in a small space is deep, great soil. The roots need to go down deep, not out wide. And that's good, because the deeper they go, the more reliable the water source is.

49

You'll need a 40-pound bag of 5-10-5 garden fertilizer. You won't need it all for this small plot, but the 40-pound bag is around twelve bucks and a five pound box is not a whole lot less. You might try to con your neighbor into building a vegetable bed and split the fertilizer with him.

And you'll need organic matter. Bags of ground bark mulch are best, the stuff piled on pallets in the megamart parking lots. At least four bags. More is better. Sawdust works if you can get it. Horse bedding. Mushroom spawn. Leaves. Anything that once grew and doesn't anymore.

Ideally you double dig the bed. That is, remove the top layer one spade deep, set it aside, and work on the bottom exposed layer. Dump at least three bags of mulch in the hole, a dozen handfuls of fertilizer (more if you use sawdust), and spade it all in. A couple of times. Wait a day and do it again.

Then put the soil you removed back, dump more organic matter and fertilizer, and spade that. If you are only half committed, you can just do the top layer without double digging, but it isn't as good. Besides, it's March; what else have you got to do?

Set the frame over the prepped ground. The spading and added organic matter will half fill the frame, but you will need to add more topsoil Fill it to the very top of the frame. It will settle.

That's the last sweating you'll do. Unless you grow hot peppers. We'll talk about that later.

Summer Bulbs

Read the directions; that's what I always say. I'm not sure why. I guess it's because that's something you are supposed to say. Federal law or something. But sometimes directions are written by idiots for imbeciles. Those plastic bags of tender summer bulbs are an example. You know—cannas, callas, tuberous begonias, dahlias and the like.

The package usually says something like, "Plant in good soil after all danger of frost is past." That works. Do that and you will have flowers. Eventually. But it is too simple. If the proper care for a plant could be synopsized in one sentence on the back of a package, I'd be out of work.

There are a lot of people who just plop these in the ground on Memorial Day and go play golf. They get away with it. Summer bulbs are pretty much idiot proof. But they get flowers weeks later than people who put a small amount of effort into it.

 Tuberous begonias will tell you when they want to start growing, and it's usually about now. What had been brown lumps all winter develop pink bumps on the top, looking very much like pimples on prom night.

You can just ignore them. Before long the pimples will turn into tiny tight clusters of baby leaves. They will wait there for two months until you are ready to put them in the ground. But you have lost two months, and flowers will be weeks later than they have to be.

Better to pot them up as soon as you see the pimples. Use a rich soil mix, like African violet soil, and set them so the top is covered an inch deep. You can start individual tubers in four- inch pots, or you can put several in a larger tray, transplanting them after they start to develop roots.

An east window is perfect, but they are forgiving of lesser lighting. Not a whole lot less, but a little. Don't take that as an excuse to

put them in the dark. Plant them outside, you know, when danger of frost is past. You'll have those big fabulous blooms in early July instead of mid-August.

Dahlias aren't so easy, because they need a bigger pot. On the other hand, they are easier, because the instructions on the label lie. You can plant dahlias out earlier than the label says. It tells you to wait until danger of frost is past because that is the only English the blurb writer knows, but dahlias can be planted three or four weeks before the last frost. That way they will bloom earlier. Earlier, but not earliest. The best way is still to start them inside if you have the room to do it. Pot them up in gallon nursery containers from the stack in the garage as soon as they start sprouting.

This is the most effort, minimal as it is, but you get a bonus. When a stem gets six or eight inches long, cut it off and root it. Plant it out when the roots are a few inches long. Now you have two dahlias.

Callas and cannas are treated the same as dahlias except you can't cut off a sprout and root it. You can plant them outside in late April or early May or get a faster start by potting them up indoors.

Not caladiums. Caladiums just hate cold soil. If you are going to plant them directly outside, you should wait not only for the last frost but a week or two longer for the soil to warm up. Or start them inside, where presumably your potting soil is warm.

So put the book down. Go check your summer bulbs. If they are budded or sprouting, you know what you should do.

It Could Be Verse

It was a small matter that first got me started—a piece on camellias. I sent it off and then read it again to find errors that hid before. They always show up once copy is out the door.

One paragraph in it jumped off the page at me. Read it yourself. See if you can see what I see:

"For a couple of years I was perfectly pleased with their small, glossy leaves and their bonsai-like habit. Plenty of plants have endeared themselves to me with nothing to offer but green."

The problem's not spelling or diction or grammar. It's rhythm. I'd written in dactyl quadrameter. Poetry!—if you can do without rhyming, for the basis of poetry's not words but timing.

So OK, I'd seen it. Who cares. What's the difference? Saw it and scanned it—forgotten. The end of it.

But now I can't stop writing lines that have metric feet. Prose comes in triplets or doublets or empty beats. (That's what I call it when words leave a rhythmic hole. You know—when reading—"da dum" or such folderol.)

So what is a writer to do. I had to give content or who would read this claptrap. I had to adapt. A column in poetry? Noo-oo-oo.

It's possible others could do such a thing. Will Shakespeare perhaps. But for me it would bring some big problems with content. I write about gardens. Obsessing on meter would strain my slim talents.

Besides, the Bard dabbled in different beats. In fives—in pentameter—lines that have feet at every second syllable. Iambic. Drop it. Much more skill is needed than I could provide. Get back to basics. STOP IT!

And yet...hmmm...I wonder. It's not without precedent. Shakespeare himself wrote of rosemary, thyme, and mint. Not always rhyming, he still got away with it. I am no Shakespeare, but let's try a little bit.

I could tell a tale of houseplants, how they know that spring is broaching. How they grow new leaves, the old ones fall. It's messy

but it tells us all of vernal chores approaching.

There's spading. No, it's still too early. Work wet soil, you make adobe. When the muse of spring calls out to grab a spade and have a bout of muscle wrenching exercise, be firm, be stalwart—NO MUD PIES!

And yet we just have to be out, to wander and watch as the stout green leaves of the tulips pop up to cajole us. We soon will have flowers, no doubt.

So there is one job you can do. You can feed those young shoots while they're new. An inch or so tall is the best time of all, but later will do the job, too.

Herbaceous perennials like to be coddled in March. A nice warm spell will wake them. A lot'll start growing fresh sprouts. Then the Arctic winds blow again killing the soft new growth.

So you should take a limb off that old Christmas tree lying behind the shed. Cover the plants that you want to sleep in the bed just a bit longer.

Cool soil will keep sprouts at bay. Exposed in April, by June they'll be bright and gay.

I give up. Gardens don't come in meter and feet. And verse is no substitute for writing all about flowers and things we can eat.

Next week I'll get back
to words that will lack
any kind
of rhythm
or rhyme.

APRIL

First Warm Days

There are many rites of passage between winter and spring. A big one, nationally celebrated, is Groundhog Day, when Bill Murray is hauled out of his hole, sees his shadow, and vows to lose 25 pounds in six weeks. But we all have our own small personal markers that tell us that winter is coming to an end.

For me it is the first ceremonial watering of the succulents. Succulents are fleshy plants with tough hides designed to survive in the desert. They are surprisingly tolerant of cold—though preferably not freezing—temperatures; deserts get cold at night in winter. But deserts are also dry in winter, bone dry. If you have succulent plants that turned to brown mush at the base and fell over, it is because you watered them in winter.

Truth be told, I do very occasionally sneak them a small sip of water between October and March, tiny sips, if they appear to be shriveling some, but I do it on the sly. See, my wife is a botanist, which means that she knows everything about plants except how to grow them. She doesn't even recognize a plant unless it is dead, dried, and glued to a file card. And since we recently put in a small greenhouse window right where she eats breakfast, I have allowed her to care for the succulents there with the strict proviso that she do nothing to them. If they need a dash of water, I do it when she is gone. I wouldn't want to confuse a botanist.

Cacti are succulents, but not all succulents are cacti. Some have better manners. I don't like cactus, and cactus doesn't like me. Whenever I've had a cactus in the house, it attacked me at every opportunity. I have had cactus run into a different room to get at me. If I must suffer thorns, I'd rather have them on roses.

Even worse than thorns are glochids. Glochids are the maddening hair-like prickles some cacti, especially opuntias, the prickly pears, have. Not big, brutal spines. Those can do little more than

55

eviscerate you. Glochids insinuate themselves by the dozens into your skin to torment you for days.

I learned the word this spring when I was puttering around my daughter's Arizona garden and tried to pick off an opuntia pad bare handed. That was not a bright thing to do, but it was sheer brilliance compared to what I did next.

I went inside and got my best gardening gloves, which I had brought with me of course, and put them on. The glochids that were in my fingers and hands are now inside my gloves. Great gloves—perfect fit, stout but supple leather, still store clean, and I'll never wear them again.

If someone gives me a cactus, I water it generously all winter.

There are many beautiful succulents without prickles, and those are the ones I grow. Though some can get huge, most are perfect windowsill size. Even the big ones are usually slow growing and remain small for many years.

An exception to that slow-growing bit is the jade plant, *Crassula portulacea* (nee *Crassula argentea*). I bought one in a four-inch pot for 69 cents, and when I finally got tired of it and gave it away, it took two men to move it out to the pickup truck. Jade plants are almost indestructible, and if yours always die an agonizing and early death, here's the drill.

First, they need a very open and fast draining soil. When they are young, you can get by on regular peat-based bagged mix, but not when they get more than a few inches high. You might consider getting a specialty cactus mix, though I hate to pay that kind of money for dirt. I use a mixture of one third regular potting soil, one third compost, and one third Perlite. You can use sand, but Perlite is lighter weight, and a big jade is hard enough to move without that added burden.

And move it you must if you want it to get really big. They love to spend the summer outside. Though some succulents will take all the summer sun you can give them, jades like a bit of midday shade. If you can find a spot that gets sun until lunchtime, that's perfect. A once-a-week summer rain will take care of watering, and in winter they might want a sip once a month or so. How easy can you get? They don't even need much fertilizer, none at all if you mix some compost into the soil.

Aside from overwatering, the most common fatal mistake people make with jades and other succulents is overpotting. Desert plants have shallow roots and want shallow pots, only half as deep as they are wide. And they also want pots on the small side. If it looks as if the jade is getting too big for its pot, wait a few months before potting it on. Procrastination is a good thing.

Small succulents are flattered by small terra cotta pots. I mulch the soil with terra cotta colored gravel from a pet store, intended for the bottom of fish tanks. It looks good and it keeps moisture away from the crown of the plant. And I like to add a stone or two for company, usually stones I've picked up on my travels. Small stones are a lot cheaper than souvenir spoons or coffee mugs or tee-shirts.

Aloe vera, the burn plant, is another succulent found in many homes. It takes the same care as jade, but it will stay windowsill size. Beyond these well known houseplants, almost every species in the plant kingdom has a succulent member. There are many succulent euphorbias, close kin to the poinsettia. There are shelves of kalanchoes in every big box store this time of year. There are crassulas and hoyas and echeverias and sedums and agaves.

They have very interesting shapes and colors. Some have distinctive flowers. Most will fit into a small greenhouse window or on a sunny windowsill and survive the care of a properly instructed and carefully supervised botanist.

The instructions are simple. Don't water them in winter. And in summer, move them outside to a sunny spot and let nature take care of them. If you are compelled to do something that makes you

feel like a gardener, you can give them a teeny bit of water soluble fertilizer, no more than half the label recommendations, once a month from May to August. If you forget, don't worry about it.

In my experience, having a couple of succulents soon leads to a collection. Of course in my experience almost any plant leads to a collection. But succulents, with their reliability and easy care, are particularly seductive.

Agaves have caught my attention of late. My daughter in Arizona has two acres of scrub land, which in her demented mind she thinks is beautiful. And on this scrub land grow thousands of agaves of all sizes, from three inch babies to man eating monsters. And as far as I know, none is protected.

Agaves are about as indestructible as a plant can get. You can dig them out of the ground, shake the dirt off the roots, throw them in a box, and take them to the post office. They will arrive days later without even noticing their hardship. This has made Christmas shopping very easy for her.

I have several agaves now. They're small enough for the greenhouse window, but some will eventually outgrow it. One that won't is Agave 'Victoria Regina', a stunning dark green with pure white edges, as pretty as a plant can get without flowers. Others are shades of blue. One is the plant that tequila is made from, though I don't expect to be brewing any for a long time.

There are hundreds if not thousands of interesting varieties of crassulas and echeverias, most of which form tight rosettes that nestle on the soil surface, like hens and chicks only better. If you buy them, you usually get one rosette, but they multiply. When you have several, it's easy to break one off and stick it in a new pot of cactus soil, watering ever so slightly until roots form. Most succulents root very easily.

That's one of the great things about them. Once you have bought a few, you don't have to spend any more money. You just have to find another succulent enthusiast. With plants so easy to propagate, trading with other collectors is a money saving natural.

If you are headed south any time soon, or any other direction for that matter, keep an eye out for small local nurseries and check out their succulents. Often a mom and pop operation will have very special plants not found in the big box stores. And they'll easily survive the trip home, probably better than you.

Planting Planning

Never go grocery shopping when you're hungry. And never go shopping for plants after a long, gray winter. You come home with a year's supply of Twinkies or an acre of marigolds.

You plan before you go to the supermarket, right? You make a list. April is the time for making a shopping list for plants, before the big box parking lots fill up with seductive six packs.

There are gardeners who make detailed plot plans on paper; there isn't a magazine article on planning that doesn't recommend that. I've done it. Not very well, but I've done it. But I really prefer to do my planning in the garden.

This involves a lot of wandering around and looking, an ideal activity for those occasional balmy days. Bulbs and perennials are popping up now, and each day I find new sprouts, new promises of summer. My wife thinks I'm idle, just wasting time, but I'm doing an important job. I'm ruminating. I'm visualizing. I'm planning. This is serious work, no matter what it looks like.

To show that I am working, I use an old Army trick. I carry a clipboard. No one questions a man with a clipboard. And I carry Popsicle sticks and orange plastic ribbon.

You can get a couple of hundred Popsicle sticks at a craft store for a buck. The roll of orange

plastic tape, with no stickum, is from a building supply store.

A patch of tulips is just breaking ground. It's a good thing I remember that they are an old variety called 'Ad Rem', because the tag isn't readable. This is as good a time to replace it as any; makes me look busy.

Most tulips dwindle after two or three seasons and eventually peter out, but these are Darwin hybrids. They actually multiply if you treat them well, and treating them well includes feeding them in spring just as they break ground. So the few bulbs I planted several years ago have become three dozen. Because they are so bright and early, I planted them in the line of sight from my chair through my study window.

That view is still there after the tulips die, though, so I need something bright in the spot. You can plant annuals directly over a bed of tulips, and they are ready to go in about the time the tulips are turning brown. As the tulip leaves get unsightly, the annuals grow up to hide them.

Red petunias, I think. I plant petunias about a foot apart, so I start plopping Popsicle sticks into the ground, fiddling with them until I get the spacing right. Ten. Two six packs with a little left over for my mistakes. Or for a pot. That goes on my list.

Behind the tulips is a blank spot up against a fence. A clematis would look great there. Another Popsicle stick. And because it is in the back, I tie a piece of tape on it so it stands out. And because I forget my best ideas the next day, I write "clematis" on the tape with a Sharpie.

Nearby is a patch of species crocus under a tree. They're almost ready to bloom, beating the more common Dutch hybrid crocus by two to three weeks. And they're prettier, too. Though the individual flowers are smaller, they multiply quickly and form a solid mat of color. Conditions under the tree are perfect for these very early flowers. They bloom and wither in the sun before the tree's leaves come out and shade the spot. Since it is shady in summer, petunias won't work. I've overplanted with impatiens, but I'm tired of them. I'm thinking of something more permanent. Hosta.

Hostas emerge late in spring. The crocus will be a mass of dead leaves flopped on the ground by the time the hosta grows up to hide them. No Popsicle stick or tape needed here. I just note it on my clipboard. Hosta.

When I plant the hosta in May, I'll dislodge a handful of the small crocus corms. I can plunk them back into the ground there, or I can start a colony someplace else. Or I can plunk them randomly in the lawn. Most spring bulbs planted in lawns are later and taller; the leaves get mowed before they ripen. But not species crocus. I'll mull that as I wander.

There is a vacant spot next to the crocus, just perfect for hellebores. They'll bloom about the same time as the early crocus. This earliest of the perennials is not seen enough in our gardens. I can buy a new one or maybe transplant a volunteer seedling I have in another part of the garden. Popsicle stick, orange tape.

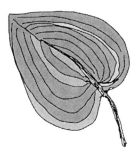

Eventually I'm back inside, in my chair, for more important work. Just what hosta, what clematis, what hellebore? I'll live with these things for years. The choice deserves more than five minutes in a nursery. I go through my books and magazines and write down three or four that I like. I'm bound to find one of them when the nurseries stock up.

Sometimes this serious research looks deceptively like casual leafing through magazines, but that is a necessary part of the process. And while I was doing that, I ran across a new introduction for this spring, *Sambucus* 'Black Lace' from Proven Winners. It was love at first sight.

Sambucus is elderberry, a small shrub familiar to our grandparents. But this one has spidery leaves in darkest purple with pale

pink flowers. It looks a lot like the fancy Japanese maples, but it isn't nearly as fussy. I had to have it. But where.

That sent me back outside. With my usual iron discipline, I wouldn't get this lovely plant without knowing in advance where it would grow. Problem. I had no ready spot for a ten-foot shrub.

This is the kind of difficulty that a real gardener loves, because it requires making a new garden space. After more intensive wandering, I decided that a square garden bed out back would look better if the end were expanded into a half circle. That would be a perfect spot for the elderberry.

I marked out the half circle with a hose and stuck a six foot bamboo stake in the ground with a piece or orange tape tied to the top. Now I could spend the next few weeks making sure that is the right spot. What looks good on Tuesday from here looks different on Friday from over there, and the orange tape reminds me to look.

'Black Lace' may be hard to find this year, but you can Google it. Be sure to include *Sambucus* in the search field. If you search for just 'Black Lace'...well, don't do it.

The elderberry won't fill the whole half circle, so I have my Popsicle sticks with me. The mature shrub will spread to six feet, but not the first year. I'll plant annuals in the space that will eventually be taken over. White ageratum should set it off nicely. I made a six foot circle around the stake with lime and started sticking Popsicle sticks in the ground.

Outside the lime circle, inside the hose, I'll plant perennials. The gray leaves of artemisia would look outstanding. I'll get a well-established gallon pot and divide it right away. Two Popsicle sticks. Maybe some lavender; I'll put a stick in the ground and think about it. And this would be a good place to put those extra crocus corms. Another stick and some orange tape. Write "crocus." Otherwise I'll forget.

Three or four weeks of this and I'll have my list. I'll go plant shopping knowing exactly what I need, exactly what I have room for. Not a thing more. Just what I need. That's all. Though to be honest, I do like an occasional Twinkie.

Cheap Stuff

It seems pretty obvious to me. Don't pay any more than you need to. Doesn't everyone agree with that?

I guess not. Otherwise people wouldn't call me the names they do. "Cheap" is one of the nicer ones; there are others that I'll leave to your imagination.

OK, so sometimes when I see a price I grab my chest and my breath comes hard. Maybe not everyone reacts quite as strongly, but the principle is the same.

For instance, I just saw some hot caps priced at $12.95 for five.  There's a chest grabber for you. A hot cap is something you put over a seedling to protect it for a week or two from the wind and cold. It needs to let light in, and it should have a vent so it doesn't overheat. A round gallon bottle that windshield washer fluid comes in, with the bottom cut out and the cap removed, does just that for little more than a couple of bucks each. And that's filled with windshield washer.

On the same page are "tomato ripening sleeves," clear plastic, 30 inches in diameter, 24 feet long, $12.95. If you cut them off in three-foot segments, it gives you eight sleeves at...oh, something over a dollar and a half each.

63

Garbage bags! We're talking garbage bags! At a dollar and a half apiece! (Excuse me while I slip a little pill under my tongue.)

Several years ago I went to one of those wholesale places that sell commercial janitorial supplies and bought a case of clear plastic garbage bags, a hundred of 'em, for about fifteen cents each. I still have over half left.

Toward the end of the season I slip them over vegetables and cut a few holes in them for ventilation. It keeps them warmer and helps reluctant tomatoes and peppers to ripen. I put a whole flat of cuttings in one to keep the humidity up. I put them over pots when I go on short vacation so I don't have to have someone come in and kill my house plants.

The one thing I don't use them for is garbage. No need for the neighbors to walk by and count the Scotch bottles.

Even cheaper than clear plastic bags is clear plastic sheeting in rolls. The thinner the plastic, the cheaper the roll, which is good because you want the flimsy stuff.

When I put out my tomatoes and dahlias in the spring, I put a cage around them, a six foot high cage made from concrete reinforcing wire. Around the bottom I wrap plastic, a foot or two high, and just staple the ends together to keep it in place. You'd be surprised how much of a head start this gives plants. By the time they grow above this plastic shield, they're hardened and ready for the real world.

Here's another example of wasting money. I've told you not to use grow lights, to just get one warm white, sometimes sold as Kitchen and Bath lights, and one cool white fluorescent tube, that they're almost as good. Well, I don't always take my own advice. I've been playing with lights, and decided I'd try some actual grow lights again, after forsaking them twenty years ago.

Forget it. Grow lights cost about twelve bucks each. One cool white and warm white (which is slightly more expensive than a cool white) come in under five for both. Grow lights can't be that good. At least I think they can't, but I'll never know. Not at that price I won't. There are things I'll pay top dollar for. I'm sure there are. I just can't think of any at the moment. But I'm not going to spend ridiculous prices for something I can replicate for ten cents on the dollar.

(Please note that in the spirit of political correctness, I got through this whole piece without mentioning anything about Scots.)

Soil

Gardeners talk about loam the way the preachers talk about grace. After listening at length and with all the attention we can muster, we still aren't sure just what it is or whether we have it.

I can't help you with grace, but I can identify your soil. Put a cup of garden soil in a mayonnaise jar (empty) and fill it almost to the top with water. Shake the jar as if you were really angry, and let it settle overnight.

You should end up with three distinct layers plus some material  floating on top. The bottom layer is sand, the middle silt, and the top is clay. The floating stuff is humus, decomposed organic matter, about which more in due course.

If you have a thick layer of clay, you have...what? Right, clay soil. And if there is a thick layer of sand? (Let's not see the same hands all the time.) Right, sandy soil. If the three bottom layers are roughly equal with a lot of stuff floating, you have—ta TAAAA!—loam. But they probably aren't and you probably don't.

Now you know, and like understanding grace, it's interesting at an abstract level, but it doesn't tell you what to do next. I will. Cure sandy soil by adding organic material. Cure clay soil by adding organic material. And if you are blessed with loam, add organic material anyway.

Soil with too much clay will clump together and squeeze out air. It dries and warms late in the spring and crusts over at the first hint of drought. Organic material in quantity opens the structure, makes air spaces, and helps break the sticky bond between the tiny soil particles.

Soil with too much sand won't hold water, and this rapid draining leaches out fertilizer. Organic matter in sandy soil acts like little sponges to hold moisture and nutrients. And in both sand and clay, organic material adds microbes and enzymes that plants need and that bring the soil to life.

Good soil needs organic matter; that's not exactly a hot news flash. Even the most inept gardener knows about humus at some level of consciousness. What many don't know is how much to use (lots and lots) and how to get it.

Leaves are a great start. You may have noticed, however, that April is not good leaf digging time unless you saved last fall's production in plastic bags. (Though if your community picks up leaves in fall, and you can find where they dump them, you've found the mother lode.) Leaves can be rototilled into the garden, but if your weapon of choice is a spading fork, you will find the job easier if you chop the leaves first with a lawn mower.

Though leaves are scarce, pallets of bagged bark mulch are appearing in every retail parking lot. It comes in several grades, and by happy coincidence, the very cheapest grade is perfect to dig into your soil. Bagged bark is too expensive for large areas, but it is great for small jobs.

Splurging on a quality rose bush this spring? Spend three bucks more for a bag of ground bark. Dig a generous four inch layer deep into the soil before you plant. Do the same for any shrub or perennial that's going to stay put for a few years; this is the last chance you get to improve the soil. If you're dividing perennials, add a generous pile of ground bark before replanting.

Some elementary math—my daughter helped me—shows that a three cubic foot bag will give you three inches of ground bark to dig in over 12 square feet of garden. That's less than 30 cents a square foot, and well worth it. So watch for sales and get as much as you can afford; it won't go to waste.

As cheap as that is, it's still steep for the big vegetable garden out back or for a new lawn. The most practical way to get meaningful amounts of humus into a large area is with truckloads of sawdust from a local saw mill. NOT truckloads of topsoil. Two four yard loads will give you four inches to dig in over a 25 by 25 foot garden. If your neighbor has a Ph.D in agronomy, he'll argue that sawdust robs nitrogen from the soil, and he's right. So what. Throw on an extra handful of fertilizer. The long term benefits are worth risking a slightly reduced harvest the first year. For some reason, the experts never make the same argument about leaves.

Plenty of humus makes the soil literally come alive. Earthworms find you and donate their castings. Friendly bacteria produce enzymes your plants crave and release nutrients locked in the soil.

These wonderful things don't happen, though, unless the soil pH is correct. Get a pH test. I know you've been sorta thinkin' about it, but this spring do it.

All of this, however, is just scratching the surface. Literally. Soil is deeper than the tines of a spading fork, and there can be some nasty stuff down there. To find out, dig a hole. It doesn't have to be too deep—a couple of feet is ample. Take a look at what your carefully prepared topsoil is sitting on.

If you're really lucky, you may have more of what you have on the surface. Less desirable, you may have gravel, a stony, sandy mixture that allows water to run through it rapidly. Your topsoil will drain well, but you'll need to take special care that it gets enough water. Worst, you could find hardpan, a yellow or gray clay that could be used to make pottery. It is impermeable to water and causes your garden to be perpetually soggy.

Now you must decide what kind of gardener you want to be. The casual planter of flowers will simply fill the hole back up and go

about his work. The truly dedicated, though, will want to bring that subsoil up to the standards of his topsoil. This is accomplished through a torturous process called double digging.

Dig a trench along the end of your garden the width and depth of your spade; set the soil aside. With the second level of soil exposed, dig in all the ground bark, leaves, and sawdust you can manage along with a handful of granular fertilizer. Now dig a second trench next to the first, putting the soil in the first trench and exposing the subsoil of the second. Fix it. Move on. At the end fill in your final trench with the soil you set aside from the first. This is backbreaking work, but your plants will thrive in the deep loam soil you are creating.

Another way to increase the depth of you good soil is to use raised beds. An eight inch high frame of pressure treated wood or stone or timbers filled with prime soil is the same as digging an extra eight inches deep. And an eight inch raised bed on top of a double dug plot is Nirvana for your plants.

The humus you so laboriously incorporated breaks down over time and must be replenished on a regular basis. An organic mulch of ground mark, grass clippings, or chopped leaves will decompose over time to keep your loam in prime condition.

Admittedly this is hard work. But it draws the line between the gardeners and the dabblers. Grace is a gift, but good garden soil must be earned.

 Soil Test

New gardens teach new lessons. And sometimes they reaffirm the old ones.

The Master Gardeners of my county are creating a demonstration/ display garden, and we had our first work bee a couple of weeks ago. Three raised beds for vegetables were laid out, and ambitious neophytes started to double dig them.

In the first they encountered the roots and stump of a tree long gone. The second yielded mucky clay that made rude sounds every time you stuck a spade into it. The third was pure gravel. This within a thirty foot radius.

Meanwhile our county agent was running around waving a two page university soil test like a cross before vampires. Ever the tactful one, I took this opportunity to point out my heretical view on complete soil tests for home gardeners, i.e., that they are pretty much worthless.

Soil tests are a great tool for the farmer. His 40-acre field is probably fairly homogeneous, and if a twelve dollar test saves him money on unnecessary fertilizer or by increasing his production by ten percent, it makes a real difference.

But most residential lots have been greatly disturbed over the years. In my yard, one bank is wood and coal ash dumped for generations. Another part is alluvial river silt, obviously trucked to this hilltop location in times long past. In one corner a redbud grows happily over the site of a former privy. Most of the rest is yellow clay with a strip of well worked soil down the middle that was once a small flower bed.

Many extension agents will instruct you to take an average, mixing small samples from several areas, but think for a moment. What is the average of ashes, river silt, and clay? And what will the resulting test tell you about treating each spot?

So I respectfully disagree with the professionals. Again.

There is one soil test, though, that every serious gardener should use and use often—a simple pH test. This will tell you whether your soil is acid or alkaline, which can make a difference whether plants live or die.

You can have a pH test done at most garden centers for a buck or so, sometimes free. But better, buy a simple kit to test soil pH

yourself. Then you can do it on the spot...and on that spot, and that spot.

Don't bother with the expensive home kits for nitrogen, phosphorus, and potassium. Get the cheap one, pH only. And don't get seduced by one of those fancy electronic meters. The cheaper ones are junk, and the expensive ones are no better or easier than the simple chemical kits.

You should make separate tests of soil pH in several locations. Don't mix and average; you never know what a former owner might have done. With a clean trowel, remove the top two or three inches of soil and take the sample from underneath. Then follow the instructions in your kit.

Most soils in the Northeast are acid, and usually an application of lime is in order. Add the amount they recommend, then test again in the fall.

An exception to the acid rule may be found near the foundation, especially a new foundation. Concrete is very alkaline, and it can leach into nearby soil. Many a home owner has planted acid loving azaleas near the house, only to have them die within a season.

One situation where you might want to have a complete test done is if a plant dies and you can't find a reason. But for most situations, spend the money a test would cost on a plant and watch it carefully. It will tell you how the soil is.

National Garden

The new vegetable garden on the South Lawn of the White House is right up there with putting a DeSoto up on blocks by the East Gate. I understand that mine is a lonely opinion.

The First Garden is, as you would expect, an organic garden. I am irked that the White House is going organic in opposition to the whole Department of Agriculture, but mildly. This White House knows its devotees, and I understand the politics of it.

The First Lady has said that the whole large garden cost about 200 dollars. That, of course, doesn't count a GS-15 to manage it and a GS-11 to wield the hoe. And eventually a sub-cabinet level guy to supervise them, but the first two nominees were withdrawn, one for using Weed & Feed on his lawn, the other when they learned he owned five shares of Monsanto stock.

Part of the cost savings came from using school children to help, which in an earlier administration would have been condemned as child labor. Here I'm going to get in trouble again, so let me first say this: By all means garden with your children. I didn't, but you should. It's good for them and it's good for you.

Let's be honest, though. Eight year olds do not significantly reduce your work in the garden. If anything, they increase it. My children were banned from my garden, and as a result both have become gardeners as adults just to spite me. Dad ain't as dumb as he looks.

Without children and without civil service staff, can you get away with your first vegetable garden for two hundred bucks? Absolutely. A lot less, even though a first garden has a big front end load. For one thing, your first garden is going to be a lot smaller than the First Garden. I nagged you earlier about that, no more than four by eight feet.

You'll need a spading fork, a good one. You can buy a twenty dollar fork, break it, buy another one. You've spent forty dollars and are still working with a piece of junk. Buy a forty dollar fork in the first place. If you're lucky, you might find one at a barn sale for five, and if it's old, better still.

Use the fork to strip off the sod. I won't kid you that this is easy, but it is one time only. Pile the sod, upside down, in an out of the way spot to start your compost pile.

You'll need ten to fifteen dollars worth of the cheapest pine bark mulch, not nuggets, three or four bags. Dump it on your plot and spade it in.

You'll want a pH test, which might cost you a couple of dollars, but many garden centers and garden expos will do it for free. They'll probably recommend lime, another five bucks. You do not need a full spectrum soil test. Don't get conned into it.

You WILL want a bag of common garden fertilizer, 5-10-5 or 10-10-10 or 12-12-12, anything that isn't lawn fertilizer with a very high first number. A 25 pound bag will cost you around 15 dollars. It used to be 40 pounds for six, but then tomatoes used to be 39 cents a pound. The fertilizer is important, because you want to get the most out of your small space. Organic favorites won't do it, and anyway, the organic stuff has to break down into exactly the chemicals in the 25 pound bag before the plants can use it.

You'll want a scrap of concrete reinforcing wire to make one or two tomato cages. If you can't scrounge it, even at night, that's another eight or ten dollars. Seeds and starts, no more than ten.

What's that all add up to? I dunno. Here's where you can use that eight year old to do the math. The total is less than the food you will harvest, even the first year. And next year the return on investment will be huge.

MAY

Sex Ed

I just ran into a curious term. It seems that a school district is teaching tenth graders how to avoid "cucurbitaceous pregnancies." Of course I knew what cucurbitaceous meant—doesn't everybody?—And I knew what pregnancy was, but I didn't understand the phrase.

Reading on, I learned that they were using cucumbers, a cucurbitaceous vegetable, to demonstrate how to use...uh...an item that when I was a lad we got from gas station vending machines and somehow, instinctively, knew how to use. Not that we ever did. Mostly we just carried them around until they made a circular ridge in our wallets. It was a symbol of hope more compelling than any religious icon.

We didn't have sex education. They couldn't spare the driver's ed car for another course. We weren't even taught about the birds and the bees, let alone...well, you know. To this day I have no idea how a chicken's egg gets fertilized.

I do, however, know something about bees and cucumbers. Like so many important things in life, I didn't learn it in school.

Cucumbers are in the same family, Cucurbitaceae, as pumpkins, squash, melons, and gourds, and many of them are cross fertile. If the bees are not careful—and let's face it, bees aren't all that bright, probably because they didn't have sex education either —they will take pollen from one crop to another different crop. So, for example, a cuke might get fertilized by a bottle gourd.

This has no effect on the cucumber, other than perhaps waking up the next morning with a sense of regret, but the kids can turn out very strange indeed. In other words, the cucumber remains unchanged, just like people, but the seeds now carry a different set of genes and, if planted, can grow into a different kind of plant.

73

I have heard people complain in some years that their cukes are bitter, and they blame it on cross pollination with something the bees snuck in. Not so. Members of this family naturally contain a bitter chemical called cucurbitacin. If too much of this compound develops, the cuke will be more bitter.

Why would some cukes produce more cucurbitacin? There is no shame in admitting that I have no idea, because no one else does either. It is probably due to growing conditions—water and temperature—so there's not much you can do about it.

If you run into the problem, most of the offensive chemical is in the top of the fruit, the stem end, and in the skin. Eat the bottom and peel it. Or plant a "burpless" variety. They naturally have less of the chemical.

I've heard similar complaints about peppers. I once got into an ink fight with an obnoxious columnist (another obnoxious columnist?) about hot peppers and bell peppers. He insisted that planting hot peppers near sweet peppers would cause the sweet peppers to turn hot. Not so, though I never convinced him.

The villain here is a chemical called capsaisin and it is potent stuff. If you have ever chopped up a lot of hot peppers without gloves, you know. Capsaisin is used in sport and arthritis rubs to produce heat.

Remember that cross pollination has no effect on this year's crop, just on the seed. It will not turn sweet peppers hot, though it is just possible that the seeds themselves might develop a little bit of a bite. But who eats the seeds?

The spawn of the peppers' and cucumbers' unprotected adventures are hybrids, a cross between two unrelated plants. And just as with people, sometimes it is accidental and sometimes it is on purpose. But for some reason, they put that in the botany class, which no one listens to, rather than sex education.

Soil Temperature

It's been a different kind of spring, which means that weather is the same as usual. That is, different. Some springs are colder than normal, some warmer than normal. I don't remember ever having a spring that was normal. In weather, normal is just a mathematical average of the extremes that we actually get.

How do you know when to plant when you have a nice 75 degree day but might have a frost next week? You don't. But there is wisdom in the adage to hope for the best but plan for the worst.

Warm days get the gardener's blood surging. That first spell in T-shirts and Tivas is exhilarating for us, but it might not be for our tomatoes. We've had the good sense not to pack the wool sweaters away yet. Tomatoes don't have that option.

There is a better way than air temperature to decide when to plant different crops, and that is soil temperature. Old timers said that you can plant warm season crops if you can sit bare bottom on the soil for five minutes. I don't recommend this procedure. Organic gardeners may favor it, but the police do not.

No one has ever been arrested, though, for sticking a thermometer in the soil. In fact, there are thermometers specifically intended to check soil temperatures. They are sold at a premium price to fools. I have one.

Get a cheap outdoor thermometer, the kind they used to give away at gas stations. Stick it in the ground so that the little bulb at the bottom is four or five inches deep. You can sit there (with your pants on please) and watch the red line go down, or you can come back in a few minutes.

 Tomatoes want soil that is at least 60 degrees, peppers and melons ten degrees warmer. You can plant them earlier, and many do, but they will just sit there and complain until their roots stop shivering.

If you want to get pushy with Mother Nature, you can hasten the soil warming with clear plastic laid on the planting bed with the

edges covered with soil. A few sunny days will warm the soil as well as sprout weed seeds and then cook the weeds. You can cut a hole and plant through the plastic or take it off at planting time.

Clay stays cold longer than good organic soil, just another reason to put effort into improving your soil. And raised beds warm up and dry out earlier still. That is why I can plant while neighbors are still stepping over puddles.

Once the plants are in the ground, though, the weather is apt to change on you. For warm season plants, it doesn't take a frost to harm them. Nights dipping into the upper thirties will set back tomatoes and peppers and basil and impatiens and others whose home is in the tropics. A couple of chilly nights, and they will sit there for a week or two to make sure it won't happen again.

Various season extenders are good to use even if you plant at a sensible time. My favorite is gallon plastic jugs such as windshield washer bottles, with the bottom cut out and the caps removed (page 63). That will give them a greenhouse atmosphere and keep them several degrees warmer at night. And they are almost effortless. For storage I run a rope through the handles and hang them from the rafters in the garage until the next spring.

Floating row cover also gives plants a boost. It also keeps the bugs off. Early in the season it keeps flea beetles away. But for plants that flower and fruit, you need to take it off in June so the bees can get at them.

Not so with leafy plants and root crops. Leaving the floating row cover on potatoes, for instance, will keep the Colorado potato beetles away.

One of the more interesting gizmos to come along in the last decade is the Wall O' Water. It's a double walled plastic cylinder which you set around a seedling, and it really works. The water

absorbs heat during the day and releases it at night. I've had tomatoes come through nights when the water froze but the tomato didn't.

Here's what you do. After you put your transplant in, cover it with an upturned five gallon pail. Slip the empty Wall O' Water over the transplant, fill the cells with water, and very carefully pull the pail out. Then you go inside, replace your drenched sneakers with rubber boots, and try to set it up again. Hint: The ground must be perfectly flat and level for any chance of success.

As a last resort I have a shed full of old sheets and comforters. Any sheet that has been in the back of the linen closet for more than ten years goes to the garden shed. On those nights when you are snuggling under the covers, make sure your plants are too.

 ## Passalong Plants

A couple of years ago I stole a book called *Passalong Plants* by Felder Rushing. I didn't actually steal it, but...well, yes I did. But I didn't mean to. Not really. It's a long story.

Passalong Plants is a book about the flowers that have filled gardens for generations, since long before Lowe's and Home Depot. And the reason these humble plants were so popular was that they multiply and are easy to divide. So easy that even our grandparents, who are stumped by the most basic cell phone, could do it. Most of them have been greatly improved with more flowers and brighter colors, but their modern counterparts are still easy.

In those days, people didn't buy plants, they shared them. Passalong plants. They would divide overgrown perennials, plop them in a cardboard box, and go visit friends. I still do that, but mostly now my friends lock their doors.

Mums can be divided every year; there's nothing to it. They should be waking up and stretching now, with an inch or two of strong growth. Just slip a spade under the clump and lift it. Tease

out three or four strong sprouts, replant them in the same spot, and water in. That's after you have spaded in some fresh organic matter and fertilizer of course.

There are many other shallow rooted plants that are just as easy—lambs ears, ivy, most ground covers in fact. That's the nice thing about ground covers. You can buy one or two, let them get settled and expand a bit, divide, expand, divide. You don't need to buy a whole flat at once.

When you lift them, the soil will probably fall from the roots. Don't worry about it. If you garden in adobe and the soil clings, there's good news and bad news. The good news is that your plants won't multiply as fast and you can delay dividing them. If that's what you want. The bad news is that they won't multiply as fast because they are not happy and are not thriving. You can decide what is best for you; I'd recommend putting some effort into improving your soil. But that's just me. Me and every good gardener in the world.

Daylilies are a little harder to get out of the ground, but only a little, and they are just as easy to split up. I still have some old fashioned lemon lilies my sister gave me decades ago. When we moved here, I dug them up, brought them down, dumped them, upside down, out back and forgot them. For a year. The next spring they sprang back to life. They will certainly survive a few hours in a cardboard box.

You can pull daylilies apart. The traditional way is to use two spading forks back to back, plunged into the center of the clump to pry it apart. But it is easier to use a stout knife and cut the clump into four inch hunks. You'll see some naked spots where you have sliced through a fleshy root, but don't worry about it.

The dig and slice method works on a huge number of perennials, daisies and phlox and sedums and yarrow and monarda and, well, the list goes on. And if I were being paid by the word I would be tempted to go on like a ninth grade essay.

Phlox in particular likes to be thinned out regularly. If the plant gets too happy and sends up a thick stand of stalks, you are inviting mildew. Don't tell me you've never had all your phlox leaves turn powdery gray. It won't kill the plant, but it is ugly. The Volcano Phlox line is very resistant to mildew, but if you have older varieties, divide regularly.

Plants like these that are ready to be divided exhibit two kinds of symptoms. Some expand out in a circle, leaving the center dead. They really need to be lifted and divided now.

Others spread out over a wide area by underground runners. If they have the room to wander, you can let them. But when they crowd other plants, it's time to dig out the attacking parts and share. If you waited too long, you'll probably need to dig up both the invader and the invadee and untangle them. Then you'll have two things to share.

Daffodils are bulbs, but they too multiply and can be divided after they bloom. Perhaps it is best to wait until the foliage dies back in June, but that isn't vital. Dig up a clump, pick out the excess bulbs, and plant a few of the biggest right back.

Some plants are "easy" to divide in the sense that it is almost impossible to kill them, but that doesn't mean that they are easy to get out of the ground. I'm thinking of large hostas, tall ornamental grasses, and balloon flower. They cling to the soil like a teen to his cell phone.

Ideally you want a backhoe. I don't have a backhoe.

I have read fairy tales in reputable magazines about how you get a friend and put a spade into each side to lift it together. Great idea. Now you have two broken spades and two people with back trouble.

The easiest way to get the behemoths out of the ground is to do it piece by piece, though that isn't exactly dead easy either. I dig a small hole beside the clump with a trowel, about 12 inches deep

and wide enough to get a small saw into. I cut the clump into manageable pieces while it's still in the ground.

This spring I got a power reciprocating saw—for work on the house, I told my wife, but I had a secret plan for it. It makes short work of cutting off six by six pieces of stubborn clumps, and a six-inch chunk won't break a spade.

Lilacs and other shrubs send up shoots a short distance from the base. These suckers are just begging to be transplanted. Dig one up and snip the root connecting it to the mother plant. Often you will get a sprout, a piece of main root, and few of the smaller feeder roots. Then it's a good idea to pot the sprout up in a nursery container of good potting soil for a few weeks. Then you can replant it.

Old lilacs may bloom less and only at the top. You can rejuvenate them by cutting out up to half the oldest trunks at the base, which will cause new free flowering shoots to grow up. And as a fringe benefit, it will also stimulate the suckers for you to pot up. You can have that long hedgerow of lilacs you've always wanted.

Many of the grand old plants are self seeding annuals, and they are really easy. Rose campion is one of my favorites—beautiful foliage and brilliant flowers—and they spring up all over the place. So do many euphorbias and sedums. Most gardeners treat them like weeds and pull them out, but why? These little seedlings won't take the cardboard box in the trunk treatment, but pot them up in three inch pots. You can put them where you want or trade them for something you don't have.

Why would you do all this? I mean, assuming you aren't a compulsive multiplier like me (I'm getting treatment). For one thing you can give them to a friend, a friend who also has some overgrown plants you want. That's why they are called passalong plants. Or you can start a new garden out by the corner of the drive, where you've always wanted one. You can do it for free, which should remove your last excuse for putting it off.

Garden Rooms

There was a time when we didn't have garden rooms. Only the English did. We had a back yard and some chairs, maybe a picnic table. I recently did a program on garden rooms, which meant I needed to think about things I had been doing for years without thinking, always a scary task.

I have always made garden rooms. It wasn't a sophisticated design strategy. It's just that I like to work on small areas, one at a time, and this way I could have at least one looking decent. Maybe.

Forced to think about what I did, I figured out that a garden room, like any room, needs a floor and walls. Maybe a ceiling, but the sky works too. Quite well, actually. Unlike a living room, the walls do not have to be high to completely close the room off from, say, the bathroom. They don't even need to enclose the area fully. But they do need to define a space.

One way to do that, a way few ever think about, is with a backhoe. Most gardeners live forever with whatever topography God or the builder left them. But half a day with a backhoe, raising this area, lowering that, can cost no more than a new couch for the living room, and it lasts longer. Long enough, in fact, that the next owner won't even think of changing it. A low wall with some stone recovered from the digging or one of the new concrete wall systems and you have a terrace.

More common are fences, hedges, large planters, and existing structures. Or a combination of these.

Waist-high fences preserve a view while still defining the space. Tall fences can block an ugly view, but you don't want a tall fence on more than one or two sides. It gets claustrophobic. And consult with the neighbors before you put a fence up; that can avoid a lot of agitation down the road.

I have two areas set off with three-foot boxwood hedges, over a hundred feet of them. It all started with one little boxwood in a four inch pot. It grew, I clipped it and rooted the clippings. The next season I had a six foot hedge started. Shearing that gave me enough cuttings to surround a whole 20 by 20 foot garden room.

I use planters and pots a lot to define areas. Just outside the back door is a little seating area around a small pool. The back of the bench forms one edge of the space, and I pile a dozen or so containers to put the garden in garden room. Looks pretty decent for six or seven months of the year. The other months we don't sit out there much anyway.

With patience and a little vision, you can create a defined space with little or moderate expense. Less so with the floor.

Personally, I just love the look of Belgian block. I know people with Belgian block patios, like old European village squares, but not me. My Scottish soul could not tolerate the hefty cost.

I did it the Campbell way. I made an edging of bricks salvaged from demolished buildings and spread a load of crushed stone. It makes a comforting crunching sound when you walk. I also laid out flat rocks from the nearby creek to make paths. Looks good in a rustic way.

Finally all you need is to furnish and light your room. Everyone is suckered into the ease of solar lights. Who can resist. You just go out and stick them where you want, right? A minute or two.

The ads and the PR copy on the box don't waste your time with the drawbacks, and there are many, not the least of which is that you can't use them in the shade, not at all.

Even in the gardening flacks' favorite phrase, "part sun," where many flowers may cling to life but don't thrive, solar lights do worse than roses. Their light at night is weak and brief, often conking out even before my wife, who keeps 19th century farmers' hours. And at their best, they are dim.

Twelve-volt systems don't care if they are in the shade. They just care about being plugged in. If you are anywhere near a receptacle, that's the way to go. Even if there is no outdoor receptacle nearby, it is often a fairly easy job to put one in. I did it myself, so you know it must be simple.

There are tungsten lights and halogen lights. Tungsten is cheapest, but halogen is better and only slightly more expensive. They give you a lot more oomph for the buck and for the volt. Plus they are made of metal, not plastic. The latest thing is LED—light emitting diode—fixtures. They're bright, but they're blue. They call it daylight, but it's blue. I like the warmth of tungsten or halogen. Your choice.

Lay the wire (leaving lots of slack for when you change your mind) and hook them up late in the day. By the time you go in to fix a cold drink, it should be time to come out, sit down, and enjoy your new room.

Tire Planters

OK, Campbell. Take a deep breath, grit your teeth, and just do it. Here goes. I think it's time we said a kind word about tire planters. There, I got it out.

I have an aunt, now a wonderfully exuberant eighty-something, who is known fondly, if discreetly, in family circles as the Queen of Kitsch. Avon bottles, glass animals, and souvenir ashtrays from Buffalo and Pittsburgh blanket all horizontal surfaces; the refrigerator is hidden behind a shield of charming magnets; there's even a deer head on the wall in the living room. I swear. Right next to Elvis rendered on black velvet. (OK, I lie about Elvis, but there really is a deer head in the living room. And every December it sports a red foil nose, leaving the impression that one of my relatives shot Rudolph.)

83

It goes without saying that tire planters flank her walk and dot her lawn. She is a typical rather than a fervent gardener, a gardener like many Americans, with a yard filled with flowers all summer, but nothing particularly exotic or difficult. Attaining and maintaining that seasonal color is a chore rather than a joy, akin to painting the trim and cleaning the screens. Yet she does her duty and her flowers thrive.

 One reason they thrive is those tire planters. This horticultural dunderhead has unwittingly stumbled upon the concept of raised beds. She doesn't know that, of course. She thinks they're just art —scalloped, whitewashed, petunia-stuffed art. That these simple constructions also provide excellent growing conditions is unappreciated.

I do not have tire planters in my front yard. What I do have, and which serves the same function, is a small area built up with stones and filled with good soil. By some inscrutable process, American society has determined that materials scrounged from a creek bed are more tasteful than materials scrounged from an old Pontiac.

I don't have tire planters in my front yard, but I do have them out back, behind the garage, in the vegetable garden. It's my dirty little secret.

Raised beds, no matter what their construction, do several good things for plants. On soggy ground they add a drier stratum of soil in which to plant. On normal ground they provide that perfect drainage demanded by some fussy perennials. In spring a raised bed both dries and warms earlier than the surrounding ground, allowing for earlier planting. And since you are adding the soil, you can have exactly the soil you want.

That is what prompted me to roll my first tire into the garden. Things like pumpkins and melons want an extra rich and organic soil to produce the best and biggest fruits. So I filled a tire with almost pure compost and planted seeds. Not only did they love the soil, the additional fertilizer I applied during the season was confined to the root zone, so there was no waste.

A fringe benefit was that the black tires absorbed heat, warming the soil, which these plants also liked. Another crop that wants especially warm soil is peppers, though I use a normal soil for them. That's the nice thing about tires. You can have heavy soil and light soil, rich soil or lean, depending on the needs of the particular plant, side by side.

I even did the potato thing. Once. You know, plant the potato in one tire. As it grows add more tires and more soil until you have a pillar of potatoes. It works, though those who have the space should stick to growing them in the ground.

Tire planters do have their place, and I say that unashamedly. Don't think of it as tacky; think of it as recycling. Who knows, as environmental chic catches on, my aunt might become a taste setter in spite of herself.

Dihydrogen Monoxide

The following just came in over the transom of my email inbox: DANGER—DIHYDROGEN MONOXIDE—THE INVISIBLE KILLER. DHMO is colorless, odorless, tasteless, and kills uncounted thousands of people every year, mostly by accidental inhalation, but DHMO has also been found in malignant tumors. Besides its deadly effect on humans, it is the major component of acid rain, contributes to the greenhouse effect, and is so powerful that it even accelerates corrosion of many metals.

That is the way a fanatic might describe dihydrogen monoxide—H_2O. Water. And like many other toxic chemicals, water has many uses in the garden.

For some tasks I use hot water. Solar heated. This is no high tech setup; it's just a matter of leaving the hose stretched out in the sun. After half an hour I have a couple of gallons of hot water for washing pots, hands and feet, and animal cages. Warmed water is also handy for filling large watering cans. Container grown tropical plants don't appreciate an icy bath on a hot afternoon. But filling the can from water warmed in the hose tempers it.

Mostly it gives me a good excuse to leave the hose out all summer and avoid that hassle of draining it, looping it, and hanging it by the sill cock every day. Unsightly? Sure, but solar heating devices are expected to be unsightly.

Most water from the hose, though, is used at ground temperature and for the usual purpose: to water garden plants. This dangerous chemical is actually used by the plants as food.

We think of plant food as being nitrogen, phosphorus, and potash, but the main elements a plant needs to grow are carbon, hydrogen, and oxygen. Bet you never thought about that, did you. The reason you never think of it is that a plant gets these elements from air and water. We seldom have to give a plant air, but sometimes we have to help out with the water, the hydrogen and oxygen.

There are three approaches to watering, one wrong and two right, so the odds of getting it right are on your side.

Let's start with the wrong one. That's the one where you take the watering can out to the garden every evening and dribble. No matter how kind your intent, this actually does harm to the plants. It causes the top quarter inch of soil to remain moist, so that's where the roots grow. What you want is for the roots to grow down deep, where the water supply is more reliable. Do not water lightly daily.

The best system is to use a sprinkler to ensure that the garden gets one inch of water once a week, including any rain that might have fallen. Put pans in two or three spots within the sprinkler radius to measure. The other method that works is to use triage, giving water in dry spells only to those plants that need it most. That would be newly planted trees and shrubs and moisture loving plants like azaleas.

Or you can choose not to water at all. Grass may turn brown, but it will green up with the next rain. Flowers and vegetables will grow, though not to their optimum. And you may lose some newly planted trees, shrubs and perennials, but that is a small price to pay to avoid exposure to the invisible killer, dihydrogen monoxide.

Animals

I have a woodchuck. My neighbor has named him. Harry. Or maybe it's Hairy.

Now, I like animals. You can't walk through our house without tripping over cats or rabbits or something my wife insists is a dog but I think is really some kind of marmot. I do not, however, like woodchucks in my garden.

Here's what I did this spring. I set out the kohlrabi and cauliflower and broccoli and put bottomless plastic jugs over all the transplants. I put the Chinese cabbage and lettuce under plastic tunnels. I spread Reemay (floating row cover) over my onion seedlings and pegged it down securely.

Here's what Harry did. He knocked the jugs off and ate all the kohlrabi and cauliflower and broccoli. He crawled under the plastic tunnels and ate the lettuce and Chinese cabbage. Fortunately he doesn't like onions. But he does like Reemay. He pulled all the pegs and dragged an entire four- by eight-foot sheet into his burrow. It must be comfy.

87

I borrowed a Havahart trap from the humane society, set it out, and sure enough, the very next morning, there was...wait a minute! Are woodchucks black with a white stripe? I don't think so.

I called the Pennsylvania Game Commission, and a very nice lady there assured me there was no problem. Skunks are gentle creatures. Approach it calmly and cover the cage with an old blanket. They won't spray unless they are agitated. And anyway, they can't spray in a small cage because they can't get their tail up. Of the hundreds, perhaps thousands of calls about trapped skunks, she had never heard of someone getting sprayed trying to release them.

This is not the first time the government has lied to me. To tell the truth I have always rather enjoyed the scent of skunk wafting on a summer breeze, but up close and personal it is a very different experience.

If you have had a similar experience, you may already have learned that the old tomato juice scrub doesn't work very well. Here's what does. Put a quart of peroxide in a bucket, add one teaspoon of dishwashing detergent (Dawn is suggested, but I think that's just product placement) and a quarter cup of baking soda. It will get all fizzy like in tenth grade chemistry and wash away the odor without turning you pink.

I let the skunk out. I don't mind skunks in the garden. They eat grubs and insects, and though they may dig an occasional hole, they do more good than bad. Except that one time.

And I eventually caught Harry, who turned out to be Harriet. I moved her several miles away and I am gradually reuniting her with her family. I found out how to trap woodchucks without trapping skunks. Woodchucks are crepuscular; they operate at dusk and dawn, while skunks are nocturnal. So just close the trap when it gets dark.

I don't have deer in my garden, though other people do. When people complain to me about deer, I just smile. You should be so lucky. Usually that isn't the answer they want.

Deer damage is perhaps the most frequent question I get. You got deer? I got solutions. They may not work, or they may work some of the time, but they work better than griping to me. I've got problems of my own.

Deer are individuals. And they're smart. What stops some deer may not stop others, and what stops some now may be ineffective next week. So you need to keep trying.

There are two tactical approaches, physical barriers and repellents. Before you go out and actually spend money on something that may or may not work, you can try the cheapest repellent, which I am reluctant to name, but it is an organic solution that comes with its own applicator. It has the advantage of low cost and ease of application, but it does carry the risk of embarrassing newspaper articles and possible jail time. Other scent repellents, equally organic and less undignified, are hair and Lifebuoy soap. The hair can be packed in old nylons and the soap hung from branches.

You can put these nostrums either around the plants you want to protect, or better still, if you know where the deer are coming onto your property, along their path. If they change their path, move the repellents.

Frankly once the deer have discovered your buffet, scent repellents don't work very well. They are most effective if they can be set out before the deer find you, I'm told, but why would you go to the trouble to put out repellents if you have no deer problem?

The next step is taste repellents. There are a couple of commercial products, Hinder and Ropel, which have their adherents. One problem with these products is that they must be reapplied regularly. One university study found they'll work better and longer if you spray the plant, wait 24 hours, spray again with Wilt-Pruf, wait 24 hours, and spray again with the repellent. That's a lot of work, but it might allow your rhododendrons to actually bloom next spring.

I am told that deer won't bother a flower bed that has cleome planted in it. It's worth a try, and if it doesn't work, at least they're pretty flowers.

Fencing is expensive, and short of an installation to rival a maximum security prison, no barrier to a determined deer. Besides, most fences are ugly.

A promising new product is deer fencing made of a fine black mesh similar to pea trellising. If you have a woodline bordering your property, you weave it through the trees. From only a few feet away it disappears. And though deer could leap over it, they don't seem to want to.

A village not far from here is very proud and protective of their fabled herd of white deer. I'm told that the sight of their ghostly presence in a yard at night is awesome. The residents don't want to be rid of them. Their only resort is to plant things the deer won't eat.

There are lists of such plants. *The Sunset National Garden Book*, now out of print but available used on Amazon and well worth the money, has a five page section. You can check it out in the library, but this is a book worth plunking your money on the counter. Sunset's *Northeastern Landscaping* has a shorter listing.

None of these are as effective as a Havahart trap. But unfortunately they don't make Havahart traps large enough for deer. And if they did, just think how many skunks it could hold.

Sweet Potatoes

It was a simple matter: plant some sweet potatoes. They had arrived right after lunch, and sweet potato slips are not something you put off.

They're sad looking little fellows, a few pieces of stem bunched with a rubber band, some withered leaves on top, maybe a thready root or two if you're lucky. I've thrown better looking stuff on my compost pile. But that's the nature of sweet potato slips, and planted promptly, they will soon recover and prosper.

They like warm soil, and up north that means raised beds and black plastic. I have two kinds of raised beds. In one part of the vegetable garden are 4- by 8-foot beds framed up with attractively stained lumber and set amid neat gravel paths. But budget and energy have prevented me from doing the whole garden that way, so half is just mounded rows, raised by digging soil out of the paths and piling it up. This is where the sweet potatoes go.

Sweet potatoes, like most plants, prefer loose soil. The bed destined for this year's crop had been sitting there for three years without intimate knowledge of a spade, and it was mildly compacted by the action of rain and gravity. Actually it was far less compacted than the average ground level garden, tramped on for a generation, but still I decided to renovate it. And truth be known, having ignored that whole section since early spring, a lush crop of weeds flourished, though "flourish" is hardly adequate to describe what was happening there.

Here is how I deal with a patch that has become obscenely overgrown. (Trust me here; I'm an expert on this situation.) First I spray with Roundup a few days before I plan to get to the job. Actually I spray one day before, but I know it takes me a week, on average, to get to the next day's work. I had sprayed last week. Though the weeds still look fairly healthy, their roots are dying, and this makes them easier to extricate.

I usually rip out the offending plants and stuff them into an empty bark mulch bag. Mature weeds with their fecund seeds don't go

on my compost pile. That's where the trouble started. I didn't have an empty bag. I had a half empty bag of ground bark mulch, though, so I decided to make up a batch of my own potting mix to free up the bag.

To make a mix for my large pots, I use five gallons each of sifted compost, ground bark mulch, and last year's potting soil along with a handful of lime and 5-10-5 fertilizer. I throw it all in a garden cart and blend with a shovel.

Uh-oh. My garden cart was full of last season's corn stalks, just cut down and waiting to be ground up for mulch. OK, so I dug the chipper/shredder out of the garden shed (half an hour shot) and pulverized the stalks (ten minutes). Now for the compost.

Uh-oh. No sifted compost. OK, I put the frame I had made of half inch hardware cloth over the garden cart and sifted a mess of compost. (A friend and I sat up late one night trying to quantify exactly how much a "mess"—as in, Go out and pick a mess o' beans for supper—was. We decided that a mess was enough to meet the immediate need plus a little left over.)

The coarse material that didn't go through the screen was enough to mulch a clematis. Did that. Cut out a bunch of the dead stuff while I was there. Back to mixing potting soil. Got that done, and while I was at it, I potted up a rooted brugmansia cutting. They grow fast and are an exception to the rule of potting up only one size bigger.

Along the way I tripped over the empty bark bag and remembered what I had started out to do. So I dug and pulled the weeds out of enough of that section to get at the first raised row. I dumped on a bunch of compost, spaded it in, and reshaped the bed. Finally I spread some black plastic over it and cut slashes every foot.

Now everything was ready. I plunged a trowel deep into the ground, stuck a sweet potato slip into each hole, and watered it in with mild fertilizer solution. A ten minute job, started about one o'clock. So how come I missed Jeopardy?

JUNE

Black

Black, black, bla-a-a-ack is the color of my true love's leaves. A bit out of tune, perhaps, but my heart is in it.

Don't get me wrong: green is fine, and red can be thrilling, but show me a black-leaved plant and I grab for my wallet.

It all started, I suppose, with the purple shamrock, *Oxalis triangularis*. I may have mentioned this plant before. Once or twice. Three times. Maybe more. The leaves are a deep reddish purple, a color catalog writers try to pass off as black, but in the center of each segment is a patch of true black.

And then came the ornamental sweet potato, 'Blackie'. I may have mentioned that one on occasion, too. At first it was a hard-to-find novelty. Now, through the rare good sense of marketers, it is available even in supermarkets and roadside tents.

'Blackie' is not like the little black dress, a stand-alone statement. It is part of an ensemble. I grow it with short red dahlias. I grow it with silvery artemisia. I grow it with Love Lies Bleeding. Well, I did. This year the cat dumped the seedling flat. Next year I'll grow it with Love Lies Bleeding again.

No container garden should be without 'Blackie'. It will grow out through and among the pots, tying them all together visually, and make the specimen plants leap out.

Even more sumptuous are the black leaved elephant ears, *Colocasia esculenta*. Once dear enough to make the most prodigal gardener think twice, they are now becoming available at prices we peons can tolerate. They don't have leaves as huge as the common green elephant ears, but they're plenty big.

'Black Magic' has a dusty-black leaf and 'Black Marble' is mottled. My favorite, though, is the imperial taro, *Colocasia esculenta illustris*, big black leaves with veins of apple green.

What a show! And what a versatile plant. It'll grow in a twelve-inch pot or it will grow in your pond (though if you buy it as a water plant it will cost you three times more). It takes sun but likes light shade.

I'll tell you how much I love these black colocasias. For the last four springs I have bought one. For the last three winters I have killed it. Yet I would still go out the next spring and lay down cash money for a new one. That breaks one of my cardinal gardening rules: if at first you don't succeed, give up. At least if it is going to cost money.

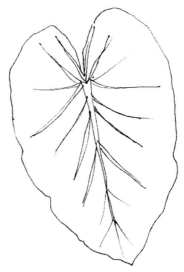

Then last spring I broke another hard and fast rule. Finding the imperial taro on sale at a good price, I bought not just my usual one, but three of them. And I tried three ways to overwinter them. Two worked. Best is to bring the pot inside, cut off the leaves just above the soil, and put it in a bright spot. It will resprout, grow feebly through the winter, and be ready to take off next season. In fact, it will multiply, so you can divide it and have a huge display.

The black mondo grass, liriope or ophiopogon—depending on which taxonomist is ahead on points at the moment—is beautiful and reliable in Zone 6, iffy in Zone 5. I've killed my share of them, but now I grow them in pots and winter them in the garage.

But I am saving the best for last, as a special treat for the two of you who read this piece all the way to the end.

Have you ever killed a Japanese maple? Come on, fess up. It is so delicate and graceful, and so fussy. If it doesn't get exactly the spot it wants, it will die a slow death.

Sambucus, the native elderberry, on the other hand, is tough as a nail. And about as charming. Until now. Proven Winners has come out with one called 'Black Lace'. Black, threadlike leaves on a rock-hardy ten-foot shrub should be enough. Add pale pink flowers in early summer and you have one of the greatest new plants in a decade. It is the Japanese maple proxy for people who have given up on Japanese maples.

For me, the maxim of a generation ago is still true. Black IS beautiful.

Frass

Frass. Can you believe there's actually a word for it?

My wife came in and asked, "What's this brown speckley stuff all over the laundry?" and I said, "Frass," and she said, "Oh." She didn't quite say, "Oh ... that's nice," but it was there in the tone. Modern accomplished women can't let a man know when they don't understand.

But it got the best of her, and after a while she asked, "What's frass? Some kind of fertilizer?" I thought about that for a moment. "Yes." No need to go into details while she was sorting laundry.

Frass is, of course, worm [expletive deleted]. You see it most easily on cabbage and other crucifers, that black stuff on the green leaves, a gift of the imported cabbageworm.

But this year it is everywhere—sidewalks and patios and especially on cars—thanks to an unusual abundance and variety of tree-devouring caterpillars. Did you have a blizzard of white moths last summer? They were the parents of this spring's elm spanworm. Then there are the ever-present gypsy moths and tent caterpillars and Bruce's spanworm (thanks, Bruce) and bagworms of various denominations.

Some very knowledgeable entomologists can identify worm species by their droppings. They can sometimes be heard whispering about a less talented colleague, "That guy doesn't know frass." Among entomologists, this passes for wit.

But there is no need for an exact identification of the critters bothering us at the moment. The treatment for all of them is the same—nothing.

These leaf ravaging beasties have already done most of the damage they will do. Spraying now will only be a waste. Soon they will pupate and emerge as moths, which don't eat; they just desperately seek out a mate. Some have only a day or two to breed before they die, or at least that's the story they give female moths. I think they learned that line from wartime inductees.

They lay their eggs, die, and you have the rest of the summer to find the egg clusters and crush them. The more you destroy, the fewer problems you'll have next spring.

And next spring you'll be ready for the survivors. Keep a sharp eye out as soon as the first leaves show. Watch for tiny caterpillars, a quarter to half an inch long. At that stage they are susceptible to just about any insecticide, but *Bacillus thuringiensis* is the poison of choice. It kills caterpillars but is harmless to everybody else. If your tongue rebels at that name, just call it *Bt* (Bee-tee).

In fact, get some now. Because even though the spring feeding frenzy is over, there are new critters coming along. The fall webworm, which arrives in summer, is eyeing your fruit trees and ornamentals. And you probably have already seen the graceful whitish butterfly that will leave imported cabbageworms behind.

Tree-eating worms have just one generation a year, but the cabbageworm can produce five or six. So they'll be after your cabbages and kale and Brussels sprouts and broccoli all season long. At the first sign of holes in the leaves, sprinkle on some *Bt*.

The trees will recover, the car can be washed, the walk swept. It's all part of the frass a gardener has to contend with.

Ponds

Only a few years ago water features were the purview of passionate and wealthy gardeners who spent hundreds, even thousands of dollars for a small piece of water. Now pond kits are sold in the megamarts for under a hundred bucks. As a result, thousands of people have put water in their landscape without any idea of what to do with it.

I can understand this. A dozen years ago I put in a tiny preformed pond. It isn't the smallest pond in the world, but it may be the smallest one without a flush lever. I had no idea what to do with it, and I subsequently screwed it up in every way possible. We call that experience. And I am prepared to pass on my experience to you, so that you will not make the same mistakes. You can make different ones.

Like all gardens, water gardens exist in a context and must fit the mood of their place. These pond liners seem to be sold with instructions that say, "Pick a spot visible from a window or deck, dig a hole, plop in the liner, and surround it with rocks." And unlike most instructions, people apparently read these. Too bad.

There are two styles of water gardens, formal and natural, and elements of the two cannot be successfully mixed.

Formal gardens are symmetrical—round or rectangular, not shaped like any inter-

nal organs. They may sit prominently in the middle of a manicured lawn. The edges are precise and fountains of mushroom-shaped water are appropriate. But few of us have homes or gardens where such water features would fit in. Beside a log cabin or farmhouse, for example, it would just look silly.

The naturalistic water garden is what most of us envision, but somewhere along the way many get lost. There is an irresistible urge to place it where we can see and hear it from a sitting area, and that often means a lawn. But really, how often do you see a natural rock-lined pool in the middle of a meadow?

Look for a spot that gives it framing, like inside an exterior corner or up against some outbuilding. Better still, look for a slope that can be carved into a mini-glen. Or a boulder outcropping or a drainage ditch or...please, anything but the middle of the yard. Take some time and squander some thought on the location.

Once sited, you want the sound of water. But ask yourself, have you ever walked through the woods and come upon a small pool with water erupting from it in the shape of a mushroom?

Just to show you that I am a flawed taste maven, I happen to be partial to those statues of small boys peeing in the pool. Not so partial that I'd actually have one, of course. What I have is a small frog spitting, which is only slightly less disgusting. Fish vomiting are also acceptable.

The ideal is a small waterfall, or a water trickle, if you are fortunate enough to have a slope leading to your pool. Admittedly this is very difficult to pull off, but the rewards are worth it. You may have to tear it out and rebuild it several times over a year or two until you get the look you want.

When I first installed my pond, I made the mistake of reading a book. As I was instructed, I dug the hole, I lined it with sand, I put the pool in and checked the level. I hauled the pool out, I dug some more, I shuffled the sand, I put the pool in and checked the level. I hauled the pool out.

I had that sucker in and out a dozen times, but finally it was level. When filled, the water came to the edge all around. The first season. That first winter the ground froze and shifted, raising one end six inches above the other. It has remained so skewed since. So much for two days of work. My advice: make it pretty level, but don't get in a tizzy over it.

Now you want a fish. Yes you do; don't argue. A fish will eat the mosquito larvae. An adequate, if undistinguished, fish will only cost only a dollar or two. It requires no maintenance. You don't even need to feed it unless you want to. It can live off the algae in the pond.

Which brings me to the Cult of Clear Water. Many people think they must spend a hundred to a thousand dollars or more for a filter. Have you ever seen a natural pond where you could see the bottom? And on the off chance you have, was that bottom made of black plastic? Some obscurity is desirable. I'm not talking about pea soup, but enough to mask the twist-off tops that crass guests and in-laws toss in.

A properly balanced pond has moderately clear water without the aid of a filter, just what you want. Properly balanced? Let's assume, laughingly, that you do what I told you and put a fish in the pond. Fish make, well, we'll call it fertilizer. Fertilizer and sunlight are a breeding ground for algae, good and bad.

Good algae is the string algae that grows on the sides of the liner and on pots you put in the pond. It masks the ugly black plastic, hides the pots, and the fish eat it. Good stuff. You want it.

Bad algae is the stuff that turns the water milky green, especially in spring. You can accept that for a couple of weeks. If you are doing things right, it goes away.

Here's how it works. As the season progresses, and if things work right, the water plants grow and absorb the excess nitrogen the fish are pumping out. And plants like water lilies spread to cover more surface, depriving the algae of sun. The pond will balance itself and the water will clear. If your water stays green, you have too

many fish or too few plants. Proper balance is easier and a whole lot cheaper than an expensive filter.

One plant that does a quick job of clearing a murky pond is duck weed. Duck weed is the world's smallest flowering plant, a couple of quarter inch leaves that float on the water surface with a half inch root dangling beneath. It's hardy in the Northeast, the minute plants sinking to the bottom in fall and popping up when the water starts to warm in spring.

It is a voracious nitrogen sucker that multiplies rapidly as the water warms to summer temperatures to quickly cover the surface. It will shorten, and in some years even eliminate the usual spring algae bloom. You don't buy duckweed. Just find a sluggish stream and grab a handful. I have a couple of tips that will save you money, tips they won't tell you at the garden center.

 As I said, my lily puddle is small, and it has a small fountain, a five-inch lead frog spitting a thin stream of water, just enough to give the sound of water. (And make me want to run inside to the bathroom every ten minutes, the downside of a water feature not mentioned in the glitzy brochures.) A small fountain takes a small pump.

I bought the smallest pump they had at the garden center for 35 dollars. After a few years it wore out. Pumps do that. Instead of going back to the garden center, I went to the local megamart and bought a submersible aquarium pump at a third the price. It works very well.

Second, water plants are needlessly expensive, a throwback to the days when only rich people bought them. A nursery will charge you six or eight dollars for a bunch of parrot feather that is essentially a weed. So take a friend who also has a water garden with you, buy one bunch, and split it.

Now you know as much as I do, maybe a little more. Go out there and get your hands dirty. Uh, wet.

Specimen Plants

I am angry with you people! I shouldn't be, I suppose. Because of you I have more money moldering in my wallet, and as a cheap gardener, that's a good thing. But it means I haven't found much to buy this spring.

Last year the selection at big box stores and most nurseries was poor. This year it is abysmal. I bought some red petunias, of course, and enough impatiens to meet the local code requirements. I passed on the acres of geraniums. But beyond that there was nothing interesting to get my juices flowing.

In previous years I have always found a pot or two or three, frequently four inch pots at about a buck an inch, sometimes larger and pricier, of "accent plants." They were unusual plants, interesting plants, often plants I hadn't grown before, and I always bought them. But you didn't. So now retailers won't stock any. It's your fault. I did my part.

Fortunately many of these special plants, sold to unwitting gardeners as annuals to be tossed at the end of the season, are really perennials. They can be kept indoors over the winter, and the next season are bigger and better at no additional cost.

Take "spikes" for example. They're really cordyline, a subtropical shrub. There are shelves full of utterly boring green spikes, or murky red for the semi-adventurous, but no Festival Grass. Festival Grass is the uptown cousin of the humble spike with gracefully arching burgundy leaves. It's fantastic for height in mixed containers. I got some a couple of years ago and still have it. It gets better every year and even looks good in winter on my sun porch.

I was lucky to have it planted in a tub with 'Silver Falls' dichondra, and even luckier to have the dichondra survive the winter along with it. 'Silver Falls' is a vine or ground cover with tiny, very silvery leaves. It's great in hanging baskets or trailing out of large patio containers instead of the ubiquitous ivy. I usually buy a fresh pot each spring, but didn't find any this year.

Another vigorous gray vine I usually buy fresh each spring is helichrysum, the licorice plant. I love the way it winds through pots of other plants. There are many varieties, and normally I get two or three kinds. This year I found only one.

Ornamental sweet potatoes will also wind through containers to provide a dramatic contrast. I did find 'Blackie' and 'Margarita', both old varieties, but the scrumptious 'Sweet Caroline Bronze' was nowhere to be seen. Maybe this spring will be better. New types have been developed and are in the pipeline.

At one stop I did see a few small pots of *Strobilanthes* 'Persian Shield'. What a plant! A four-inch pot doesn't do it justice. Kept over the winter, the following season it will grow into a three foot shrub with large almost neon leaves in purple and lavender and black. I didn't get one. The 'Persian Shield' I got eight years ago is still going strong.

Same story with the black colocasia, imperial taro, the black elephant ears. I saw it in several places this spring, probably because I don't need to buy a new one. This is a stunning container plant as well as a fine water garden plant, but if you buy it as a water plant it will cost you twice as much.

I saw my beloved purple shamrock, *Oxalis triangularis*, only in grocery stores around Saint Patrick's Day. I found none of the special coleus, just six packs of fifty year old varieties. Summer bulbs in plastic bags were almost nonexistent. Patio dahlias —nada.

One More Plant

My annual excess plant sale is now a couple of weeks past. To those proto-gardeners who tell me, "I just don't have room for one more plant," I have this to say: Ththhhppbbbbbffttt! There is ALWAYS room for one more plant, and one more after that.

I never sell my driveway out down to the pavement. There are always some plants left over. And the many leftovers are now in the ground, finding places in garden plots already stuffed like a Thanksgiving Day gullet. (But there is always room for a piece of pie, isn't there.)

People think of gardening as a process where you plan what you want, buy and install plants, and then you're finished. When a new plant leaps off an endcap into your cart, you don't even think of that plot because it is "done." Take those foundation yews. One weekend of work and you're through, right? But there is still room there for half of the New York Botanical Garden.

For starters, wouldn't those dull green blobs look better with a solid row of red petunias in front? Or white impatiens? There is probably room to just plunk them in, but even a worst-case scenario requires nothing more than digging six or eight inches further out. And doing this just as nurseries are giving away flats of annuals for pennies.

 Now take another look at the fall bulb catalogs. You could wait until the bulb displays show up in the stores, but catalogs are better for several reasons. First, if you wait, you won't do it. Remember last year? Second, store selection is erratic and always slimmer than catalogs. And finally, if you want large quantities of one kind of bulb, and you do, catalogs offer quantity discounts.

The big blooming tulips are seductive, especially when pictured as an individual blossom, but smaller flowers often make a better mass display. And usually cheaper, too. Think of the botanical tulips or miniature daffodils. Or my favorite, species crocus, which will provide a solid mat of bright color.

The first fall frost will kill impatiens, and you can plant the spring bulbs. Petunias, though, will keep blooming well into fall,

especially if you cut them back by half in August. But no problem. Just pull the stems aside and plunk the bulbs in under them. This is perhaps the one instance where a dibble is useful.

Next spring you'll have big color, and just as the bulbs begin to wither, the megamart parking lots fill up with petunias again to plant over the fading bulbs to hide the browning leaves.

Don't like a few minutes work in spring and fall? Plant a groundcover, almost anything but ivy. (Though ivy has its place, you don't want to spend the rest of your life pulling ivy out of the shrubbery.)

The bright leaves of *Lamium* 'Beacon Silver' would set off the dark evergreens. Or creeping phlox will provide a colorful carpet in June and a dense and dignified weed barrier the rest of the year. If you see anything with the Stepables tag, you won't go wrong.

Added plants don't have to be short and in front. Clematis, according to anything over a paragraph ever written about them, like to have their feet in the shade and their heads in the sun. In other words, behind yews. You just need a trellis, which should also be on sale shortly.

Sometimes you don't even need a trellis. Clematis love to grow up through open branched plants like small trees or large roses. Think about it: One spot, two plants.

There were castor beans left over. Huge as these get—six feet or more—they take only six inches of ground space. There is always room for castor beans. Just keep in mind that they are poisonous, so don't eat them.

In fact, there is always room for anything. Get out to those nursery sales and squeeze in some new plants.

Edible Flowers

Give a person fruit, like an apple or a tomato, and they'll thank you. Serve them leaves, like lettuce, and they'll eat it. Roots, like potatoes? Delicious. Seeds, like rice and walnuts? They love 'em. Fungus? Sure, pile them on that pizza. Flower buds like broccoli and cauliflower? Absolutely.

But put a flower on their plate and they look at you as if you just served them up a hair ball.

Plants don't know whether they're vegetables or flowers. This is an artificial division we made thousands of years ago, and over time the boundaries have become iron clad—in our minds, at least. But there is no logic to the system, only tradition.

What is the difference? Are some plant families food and others ornament? No, petunias and tomatoes are in the same family.

Is it that vegetables are plants that taste good and flowers don't? Just one word will demolish that reasoning: Brussels sprouts. OK, two words.

Toxicity? Are veggies safe and flowers poison? Nope. Potatoes and tomatoes and rhubarb, among others, can make you sick, but all parts of the nasturtium are edible. And better than Brussels sprouts, too.

It is simply the purest form of prejudice: arbitrary prejudice. So in the name of PC, let's eat some flowers.

Nasturtiums are the obvious starting point, not only because they're pretty and easy, but because they actually taste great. The spicy flowers mixed into a salad add zest like cress, but they're prettier. And as a garnish on a potato salad they're a lot more interesting than the clichéd egg slices. Better for you, too.

Why do we decorate cakes with calorie-packed fake flowers made from pure sugar when the back yard is full of low-cal violets? Remember eating violets as a kid, how sweet they were? That was before we were told that we shouldn't eat flowers for some reason. Add some rose petals to the icing for color contrast.

Most culinary herbs have edible flowers with the same flavor. Basil, borage, chives, hyssop, lavender—all have flowers. In many cases the flowers are a milder version of the leaf flavor, a bonus for cautious cooks.

Calendula is called pot marigold because it was used in the Middle Ages for cooking; that is, they put it in pots. The petals have the added benefit of adding a rich golden color to food. For that reason they are great in omelets.

Out in the vegetable garden you may have noticed flowers, too. Squash blossoms can be stuffed or deep fried. Bean flowers taste like beans.

One of my favorites is scarlet runner bean. What a plant. Fast growing, beautiful, full of hummingbirds. The fire engine red flowers come on all season long, so you can sprinkle them on otherwise boring green beans for contrast.

There are a couple of caveats, mostly just common sense. First, don't experiment. The garden can be a treacherous place, and you should eat only flowers that are known to be harmless. Don't eat flowers that have been treated with pesticides. And that usually means that you should eat flowers only from your own garden.

Lastly, when you're picking violets and dandelions, try to find a spot that the dog doesn't know about.

Terra Cotta

Different people are blessed with different gifts. Mine happens to be a talent for taking a prosaic and simple subject and making it hopelessly complicated. Flowerpots, for instance.

A lesser luminary will tell you that all flower pots should have holes in the bottom. Otherwise they're not pots, they're bowls, and you are certain to kill anything planted in them.

He might dip into the plastic vs. clay debate. Plastic pots are cheaper and lighter than clay, and they don't dry out as fast. But clay "breathes," which makes it better for plants that need air at the roots. And heavier clay pots are less likely to blow over in a summer storm.

Having said that, though, traditional garden writers wander off to prune their roses. Not me. I can go on for paragraph after paragraph on terra cotta alone.

There is something "just right" about terra cotta pots. I like the heft of them, I like the feel of them. Especially I like the way they look bunched together. Six or seven or eight terra cotta pots, different sizes, different shades, different shapes, some plain, some elaborately decorated, brand new and vintage, made in Italy

and China and Mexico, and they always look as if they were intended to be a set.

Tuscan pots from Italy are the king of the genre, and their price sometimes reflects it. Believe it or not, I've seen Tuscan pots priced in four—count 'em, four!—figures. And if Tuscan is king, Mexican pottery is the peasant. The price is good, but buy with care. I have had Mexican pots actually dissolve in the rain.

An impressive newcomer in the market is terra cotta from China, handsome, sturdy, and dirt cheap. (Well, terra cotta IS dirt, after all.) I have had several for a few years now, long enough to know how well they hold up, and I absolutely love the look of them. Best of all, I love what they have done to the Tuscan prices. Faced with pots of near equal quality at a tenth the cost, the Italians have dropped their prices.

I have about a ton of terra cotta, and the collection grows every year. I've bought terra cotta pots from farm stores and tony shops and ateliers and megamarts and yard sales at prices ranging from a few pennies to lots and lots and lots of pennies. Over the years I've learned a little about them.

Like everyone, my first clay pots were the standard, machine made frustums. Frustum is solid geometry talk for something that is a segment of a cone—pot shaped. Flower pots are shaped like that for a reason. If the soil expands from freezing or vigorous root growth, the soil ball will lift up. That's how it's supposed to work at least. In a straight sided pot, or even worse, a pot rounded in at the top, expanding soil will break the pot.

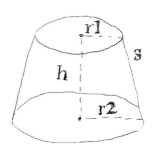

Another advantage of a frustum is that it is easy to get plants out of them when you need to put them in a bigger pot. Straight pots are more difficult, round pots are impossible. I love the look of round pots in an array, but I use them only for annuals and summer bulbs that won't vex me later.

The standard model frustum is as wide at the top as it is tall. Azalea pots are shorter than they are wide, perfect for shallow  rooted plants like azaleas, begonias and cactus. Bulb pans are shorter still and are traditionally used for forcing tulips and daffodils.

My stack of inexpensive clay is gradually being reduced by attrition to a pile of worthless clay as winter weather pounds it into terra cotta spalls. The moisture in the clay alternately freezes and thaws, breaking the pot into small particles. But some clay pots seem to be frost proof. I wondered why this was and how to tell the difference, so I asked a friend with a Ph.D. in flower pots. I'll pass on what he told me, mercifully edited down.

Two things affect whether a pot will flake: the extent to which the raw clay is worked and the firing temperature. Well-kneaded clay is more resilient. And pots fired at 2000 degrees are tougher than those fired at lower temperatures.

And how do you tell the difference? You can't. It took him about eight pages to say that.

The only useful information he passed on is that handmade pots are much tougher than machine made ware, and looking back, I have to agree. I buy pots from a local artisan, and I've never had one flake. That's the good news. The bad news is that handmades cost three or four times more than the common stuff. But if you splurge on just one...well, maybe two...each spring, or for special occasions, after a while you will gather a collection that would give you shooting chest pains if you added it up.

After a pot has aged for a while, it may or may not develop a coating of moss. Some kinds of clay seem to be better at this than others, but like flaking, I don't know of any way to tell without trying them. To hasten the process, swab on diluted buttermilk or yogurt. You can even put these mixtures in a blender with some moss gathered in the woods. Whatever you try, though, nothing will work if the pot is not given conditions that favor moss, shady and damp.

The white stuff that forms on pots is usually excess fertilizer salts and hard water residue. I call this patina and cherish it, because that's easier than trying to clean it off. If you must have pristine pots, though, soak them overnight in a ten percent chlorine bleach solution, scrub with a wire brush, and wipe them down with linseed oil.

Pots can grow moss and sweat minerals because they are porous, they absorb water from the soil in the pot. If you put potting soil in terra cotta that is new or has been stored dry, it will take the water from the outer layer of soil; that layer will shrink and pull away from the pot. You don't want this. When you water, the water runs down the space in the sides instead of into the soil. So always soak dry pots before planting.

Planting what? Just about anything. Certain plants look wonderful in certain pots, but that is a personal judgment. But for starters, try this. Next spring find a pot you love and pop in a single nasturtium seed. In a sunny spot on the patio or deck it will quickly sprout and tumble over the side and grow into a work of art. Then imagine what half a dozen different pots, with other easy plants, would look like.

Having rhapsodized about terra cotta, you might think that I disdain the humble plastic pot, but I don't. Like most gardeners, I have stacks of them piled in the garden shed in every size except the one I need at any given moment. They are a healthy home for most plants, but not particularly handsome.

That's what jardinières, or cachepots, are for. Jardinières are decorative containers that serve two purposes. They dress up a plant, which may actually be growing in a really ugly pot, and they protect the floor or table where the plant sits.

Terra cotta pots naturally look right together, but with jardinières you need to make an effort. For example, on the sun porch I have jardinières that are mostly white.

White cachepots come in a large variety of sizes and shapes at moderate prices, and they fit in with the white-painted wainscoting and ferny paper.

The smaller sun porch off the kitchen is painted in earth tones. There the plants sit in copper. Copper is not cheap. For this article I considered adding up what I've paid over the years for copper pots, but I decided I didn't want to know. For someone with one or two special plants, though, the price is bearable. A similar effect can be had with brass, which is both cheaper and easier to find.

Other gardeners have other preferences. McCoy pottery from earlier in this century can be found at reasonable prices. Tacky in the '30s, it's collectible now. Old crocks in perfect condition go for an arm and a leg at auctions and antique stores, but those with slight imperfections are ten cents on the dollar. Their neutral tones are perfect to set off well-grown plants.

Many tender plants in plastic pots spend the winter in these decorative containers. But more important, in summer I fill plastic pots with inexpensive annual flowers and grow them in the sun near the hose. For a company occasion it is a quick job to move them into the jardinières already positioned inside.

New readers may have doubted I could carry on so, but the veterans are used to it. Next time we meet, we can talk about concrete and wood and fiberglass and bamboo and glass and stone and hypertufa. Especially hypertufa. I can hardly wait.

Oxalis Triangularis

It is time to revisit *Oxalis triangularis atropurpurea*. I've mentioned it in passing several times, but you have not been sufficiently bored. I figure an entire column on the subject should do the job.

You remember. It's the "shamrock" plant with the maroon leaves and lacy lilac flowers. It is drop-dead gorgeous, yet easy enough even for my sister-in-law to grow.

It isn't really a shamrock, of course. The true shamrock, *Trifolium repens,* is a noxious lawn weed, white clover. Sometimes you'll see white clover sold as shamrocks around St. Patrick's Day, but that's just marketing. So is selling oxalis as shamrocks. Growers have learned that even the Irish won't pay top dollar for a pot of weeds.

This fairly new plant has been hard to find, but this spring I've seen it in four inch pots in just about every nursery I've visited. Nurseries are finally catching on.

So here is the first thing I want to tell you about it. Buy this plant. For those who have never, ever taken my advice before, have never remotely considered such an aberration—and that is just about everybody—take it now. Buy this plant!

This is a pot plant that will thrive under inept care. It can spend the summer on the deck or porch in its four inch pot and be happy, or you can pot it up a size or two if you want to do something proactive. Give it sun or shade, feed it if you wish, water regularly but don't panic if you forget.

Eventually time or abuse will force it into decline. If it hasn't happened by fall, stop watering and put the pot in the basement until the top withers and dies. But that is not the end, just the beginning. The patio plant will reincarnate itself as a houseplant.

Once the top is dead, knock the soil out of the pot and you will find a clump of corms that look like several lawn grubs having an orgy. Break up the party.

You started in spring with one corm in a four inch pot. Now you have half a dozen. Break the bunch apart and plant the corms evenly spaced in fresh soil in an eight inch pot. Water lightly and put it in a sunny window. Or a not so sunny window.

What was a nice little plant in a four inch pot turns into a glorious display in a larger container. The dramatic foliage forms a perfect mound and it flowers reliably in the middle of winter. An occasional feeding with a 15-30-15 soluble fertilizer will help it along.

In early spring do what you did in fall. Let it dry out and go dormant. It is time for the third reincarnation, this time as a bedding plant.

When you knock the soil out of the pot, you will find that each individual corm has again formed a small clump. You can't stop them from partying. Break them apart as before.

This oxalis is easier to plant in the ground than marigolds. I shall save for another day my rant on preparing the soil, except to say that anything grows better in good soil. Once your bed is fertile and friable, just tuck the tubers in an inch deep and ten inches apart. They'll grow in sun or shade but do best in half sun. And to be honest, though I hate to encourage you, they'll grow well in just about any soil.

Their striking dark leaves look best contrasted with something light. I put some among the gray leaves of a patch of lambs' ears. And a large bed under a pear tree always stops traffic.

Their one shortcoming is that they are not winter hardy where I live. So when the first fall frost knocks down the foliage you must dig them up. When you do, you will find...what? That's right—each corm has formed a small clump. Pot up a few for the winter, but the rest must be stored.

I keep mine over the winter in a mesh onion bag hanging from the joists in the basement. They do need some air, because during the growing season they form a second kind of tuber, a white, fleshy carrot-like root, which shrivels away during storage. In a closed bag it would get moldy.

This is a duffer's plant because it is so easy, and a connoisseur's plant because it is so beautiful. Just one time do what I tell you: Buy this plant.

Cheap/Fast/Good

Do you know about the cheap-fast-good triangle? One leg is labeled good, one is cheap, one fast. Got it?

Here's how it works. With anything you want to accomplish or acquire, you can have any two adjoining legs, but almost never all three. You can have something good and have it fast, but it will cost you dearly. Or you can have something fast and cheap, but it won't be very good. Something both good and cheap is possible, but it takes time.

Take Minute Rice. It's fast, though not quite as fast as its trade name indicates. It's pretty good, even if those who pay big bucks for their imported French cooking pots might argue the point. And at a couple bucks a box you might even think its cheap, but for the same money you can get ten times as much Hour Rice.

This simple device applies to just about everything you want to do in life, especially in the garden and landscape. You are entitled to choose whatever two legs you want, but you need to be aware of your choice and particularly what it doesn't include.

You can see an example in the enticing full page advertisements that show up on the back pages of Sunday magazines, with smarmy drawings, not photos, promising fast shade for a few bucks or a quick screen hedge for only pennies a foot. Fast and cheap, but keep in mind what is left out.

Heres a rule of thumb: Trees that grow fast do not grow strong. Take the Bradford pear. Actually, don't take the Bradford pear. Beautiful flowering yard tree, fast growing, millions were planted a decade or two ago in raised ranch developments. People were

115

happy until there was a crash, often in the middle of the night, when they fell over in a light wind or moderate snow load. I saw them offered at my local big box store this spring, and they are gone now. I hope you aren't one of the people who bought them.

Different people give different legs different values. Advertisers and marketing managers know that many Americans want instant gratification, fast. Their choice is commonly either fast and good or fast and cheap.

Fast and good is expensive, but it is more and more the combination of choice. It means buying full size specimen plants, instant impact, instead of cheaper, smaller plants that will grow into specimens in two or three or four years. And at the high end it is hiring a professional landscaper to come in and create a mature dream garden effortlessly and overnight. That is serious money. And it isn't gardening.

I always buy small plants, and no, not because they are cheaper. Well, not only because they are cheaper. Small plants establish better to their new conditions. A plant that has grown large and lush in a greenhouse with perfect container soil is not going to be delighted when it gets plunked into whatever you have to offer it and whatever weather comes by. It will sulk, and it may die.

Smaller plants, like children, are more adaptive to new conditions. In some cases a small plant, after two or three years, will outperform the big expensive one. Good and cheap. The only thing you sacrifice is time.

Besides, the really good part is that you get to watch it grow. If you have children, would you rather start from the beginning or adopt a teenager. OK, bad example. No one wants to start with a teenager. The point is that the joy is in watching them grow. And in that process, you learn. With kids and with plants.

 New gardeners often go for fast and cheap. That's why the parking lots of big box stores fill up with truckloads of six packs of petunias and impatiens in spring. Fast and cheap. Stick

them in the ground on Memorial Day and you have plenty of flowers by the Fourth of July for a buck and a half a six pack.

Or worse, the current trend is four inch pots of annuals in full bloom when you buy them. Just plop them in the ground for an instant garden. Wholesalers pot up the six packs, grow them on for three more weeks, and sell them at ten times the price per plant. Fast. Not cheap, not good. Sometimes you get only one leg of the triangle. Americans want—the survey shows!—instant gardens with no effort. It is a little sad.

You know which leg I totter on—cheap. And if you are charitable, you might also allow that I like good. That makes my choices easier. I sacrifice fast, but in my mind that is the least important leg.

With perennials, the saying is that the first year they sleep, the second year they creep, and the third year they leap. People who buy an instant perennial border miss those first steps.

The experts tell you to plant perennials in odd number groupings of at least three or five. Its a good idea, eventually, but you don't have to start with several identical plants. I buy one, plant it, and a couple years down the road I divide it. Then I have three good plants, sacrificing only time.

For the serious gardener, or serious wannabe, this has fringe benefits. Instead of spending money on five identical plants, you can buy five different plants for the same money. Here's what you do, the perfect argument for cheap and good.

Pick out several perennials you want in your finished border. Buy one of each. Now you have only a fifth of the eventual border to plant, only a fifth of the ground to prepare, and you can do it right. Dig deep, add plenty of organic matter. Oh, go ahead and double dig it, getting down into the subsoil. You can do that when you have only 20 percent of the garden to worry about. It's not easy and its not fast, but it is very, very good.

117

Put in your one-each plants. You'll have a nice garden. Small, but nice. And you can observe how the plants grow, how big they get, how you screwed up their placement. In short, you learn.

In a year or two, after your muscles have recovered and you have enjoyed your small garden for a while, you can dig up and properly prepare the next segment. Divide the plants you already have. It won't cost a penny. Now you can put multiple plants together, like the experts tell you.

And it gets better. Now your muscles are in even better shape, so you can tackle a bigger part of the new border. And your plants are doubling or more. And you are learning even more, so by the time you have the whole project planted, after a few years, you have it planted right. Good. And cheap.

For trees and shrubs especially, my motto is: the smaller the better. Or as some might unkindly observe, the cheaper the better, but that is only a happy coincidence. Even when I'm scrounging plants from others for free, I prefer smaller plants.

On rare occasions cheap and good and fast come together. Like in July. The planting and buying fever of spring is past and nurseries know it. They have some trees and shrubs and perennials in containers, and they have noticed that the crowds of May have dwindled. It's mark-down time. Think about that border you were considering in April and never quite got around to. But don't use the sale prices as an excuse to buy more than one plant of each variety.

Cheap and good makes for a solid stance. Fast is just a matter of time. Time will pass regardless of how much money you spend.

Tomatoes

This is the time of year when we notice that those tomato transplants, cute six inch babies a month ago, are taking over the garden and reaching out toward the neighbors. The decision on how to grow them, which should have been made when they were set out, can no longer be delayed.

There are three ways to train tomatoes: sprawled, staked, or caged.

Sprawling is the default position. Do nothing and they will spread along the ground. The advantage of this method is low maintenance. You can't get much easier than doing nothing. The down side is that they take up a lot of room and half your tomatoes rot on the ground while the other half get chomped by various critters.

That is why generations ago people got the idea of tying the vines to stakes to keep them off the ground, thus beginning the endless argument: to sucker or not to sucker.

Staking and tying require constant attention. Almost daily you must go out and tie up errant vines. Miss this chore for a weekend and they reset to the default position.

As if this is not sufficient effort in itself, followers of the staking cult insist that you sucker. I used to think that suckering was convincing other gardeners to stake their tomatoes, but it's not. It is the tedious exercise of removing the suckers, small new stems that materialize overnight in the junction of the main stem and every prominent side branch.

Ask them why they do it, and they will explain that their grandfather did it that way. But there is actually one good reason to sucker tomatoes. It will prod the plant into producing an earlier crop, though there will be fewer tomatoes. If you want the first tomatoes on the block, plant an early variety and attend to it daily—stake it, tie it, and sucker it—but there is no point in doing the whole tomato patch that way.

Which brings us to caging, the only rational method. It involves putting a tall frame of wire or wood around the plant, so that it grows up through and supports itself.

119

The problem with this method is that inexperienced gardeners buy those wholly inadequate hoops sold in garden stores or megamarts and think they are a cage. They are not. They're as useful as a two-foot balsa wood crutch.

To get a decent tomato cage, you must make it yourself. You can use sticks and string or wire or fencing, but the very best are made from concrete reinforcing wire, heavy wire welded in a six inch grid in rolls five feet high. You can sometimes find pieces left over from a construction job, a small job where there are no guards. Or you and your neighbors might want to split a roll purchased at a building supply.

Caged tomatoes are easy to care for and very heavy yielding. In some years I have an outside shell of leaves surrounding a solid column of tomatoes.

Caged tomatoes require little work. To help the yield, they should be fertilized once every two or three weeks with some 5-10-5. And in mid-August it's a good idea to snip off the small, newly formed tomatoes. You know they wont ripen, and you want all the plants energy to go into the ones that will.

Or you can root prune. That involves cutting the roots in a circle a foot out from the stem by shoving a shovel into the ground.

Or you can do like the old joke. Something about ripe tomatoes and cucumbers and flashing. I forget how it goes, and that's probably just as well.

Tools

There are gardeners, I am told, who get by with just one spading fork, just one garden rake, just one trowel. How sad. I'm told they get by, no problems, but I don't understand how.

I work on the principle that if I have several rakes, I'm more likely to find one when I reach for it. Though my garden is not large, it is plenty large enough to lose tools. Auctions and yard sales allow me to augment my arsenal without crippling expense.

Occasionally as I rummage through others' unwanted goods, I find a real prize, usually at rock bottom price because no sane person would want it. Like some sort of surgical device I picked up. It's a stainless steel rod, maybe 3/8ths of an inch think and a foot long. One end is spatulate, like a flattened spoon, the other gently curved, like a hockey stick. I have no idea what its original use might have been, but whenever I give a demonstration with nurses in the audience, they giggle. I guess I don't want to know. But the moment I saw it, I knew I had to have it, even though less prescient browsers had passed it by.

It is THE perfect potting-up tool. When moving a plant to a larger pot, that pot should be only slightly larger, yet the new soil packed around the outside must be firm. This medical instrument does that job superbly. And being of surgical steel, after several years in the garden it still looks as if just came out of the box.

 There is a really easy way to repot a plant in a plastic pot. Find a new, slightly larger pot and dump a handful of soil in the bottom. Take the target plant out of its own pot and set the plant aside. Put the old pot inside the new one and pack the soil around the sides. When this is done, slip the old pot out and drop the plant in the resulting hole. Voila. Perfect fit and no root damage from the packing operation.

This trick works about fifty percent of the time. That is, it always works at home, but it never works when I'm demonstrating it in front of a group. Fifty percent. If you don't do presentations, you should have no problem.

If you have several overgrown plants of different sizes, you now take the next smaller one, pot it into the container just vacated by the first plant, and on down the line. You can repot a number of plants that way, and you only needed one new pot.

There are many things gardeners use to pack that soil—dowels, silverware of different sorts, even fingers. Whatever works for you. But if you see a yard sale at a doctor's house, stop.

Another yard sale find was an entrenching tool. I managed to get through three years of service to my country without any close association with this ubiquitous military utensil. Now I use it constantly. This short, smallish shovel is great for very unmilitary service in the perennial bed. Planting a perennial grown in a gallon or two gallon pot is too small a job for a big shovel, too large a job for a trowel. It's a job for an entrenching tool. And the stubby handle allows you to wield it in a crowded bed without knocking over all the plants behind you.

Then there was that rake I found with no handle (page 42). Twenty five cents. It was a perfect match for a broken handle that had hung out in the garage for several years. I now have a garden rake with a two-foot handle for those little jobs in the raised beds. If they made a tool for this purpose, which they don't, it would cost twenty bucks or more.

There's a lesson here. Maybe two. Don't pass up a yard sale offering just because it appears useless. And if you hold a yard sale, pray that I stop by.

Small New Garden

There are people who want A garden and people who want TO garden, and I'm never sure which kind I'm talking to. Because they lie. They lie to me and sometimes they lie to themselves.

I have many friends who think they like TO garden, but they don't. Their gardens are always slipping, and they complain that they just don't have the time to do what they really, really want to do. They do. Someone who wants TO garden makes the time. They let the other things slide. Ask my wife if you don't believe me.

Which are you? I have a little test. You won't need a pencil. You'll need a spade. We're going to make a small new garden, and we're going to do it right. It's pass/fail. If you finish the test, you pass. You may even be a real gardener, or at least on your way to becoming one.

July is a good time to test this. Even the most casual proto-gardener can get caught up in the frenetic spirit of spring. They're out there weeding and planting and thrashing around, and they think they are enjoying it. By July winter is long forgotten and the thrall of dirty hands has become drudgery.

Not for my kind of gardeners, though. For us the joy is in the process, the doing of it, with the hope of beauty sometime down the line, but that is secondary. July is when you find out whether your focus is dirty hands or pretty flowers.

For one thing, plants are really cheap. Its the Christmas shopping model. Smart people shop in October, really smart people in January. Gift packs of sawdust sausages and rubber cheese are not going to be any the worse for sitting in the spare bedroom for eleven months.

The same is true for six packs of petunias, though the time frame changes. Smart ones buy spring plants in May. Smarter ones go shopping in July. Retailers can't put a six pack of petunias or a four-inch New Guinea impatiens back in the stock room to await the crowds of smart people next spring. They have to sell them or pay money to the Dumpster people to haul them away. And besides, they are tired of watering them. Or to be more precise, they are tired of paying people to water them. The few six packs of annuals that are left, the four dollar specimen plants, even the perennials, are going for pennies on the dollar.

OK, they don't look so good. Clearance plants are hardly the lush, blooming seductresses the smart shoppers bought a month ago, only hours off the truck, at ten times the price. But you'd be surprised how quickly they will revive given fresh soil, good light, and a dose of blue water. Not the blue water in the toilet, but the blue water of a liquid fertilizer.

I have heard the half committed say, "I don't have room for any more plants." Such people are the Stepford spawn of pretend gardeners. There is always room for more plants. That's what this

test is for. We're going to make the room. As long as you still have grass to mow, there is room for a new garden plot.

Wander through the house and look out the windows. I know, with absolute certainty, that there is at least one view that would be dramatically improved by a huge splash of color. And if you pass the test, windows that you have always ignored will draw your eye and a smile every time you pass.

Most people, given a marked down flat of flowers, will plant them up next to the house. But ask yourself: Do you spend most of your time outside looking in? Or inside looking out. Right. So your color splash will need to be away from the foundation, maybe way out at the property line. At a distance a flower or two is hardly noticeable, but a couple dozen make an impact.

This may involve digging a new bed, but there are many advantages to doing it now. First, remember that you are going to plant all these annuals in a bunch, not spread out, so you don't need a big bed.

Second, they are going to die in October no matter what you do. That means that you need to do a good job improving the soil in the new bed, but not a great job. Spade it up, throw in a bag or two of ground pine bark mulch and some fertilizer, spade through it once again, and plant. Water stale plants in with a liquid fertilizer solution and they'll leap into growth.

There is an extra credit portion of the test. The deeper you dig and improve any soil, the better the plants will grow, period. I have given plants from my garden to friends, even friends who were basically good gardeners, and they have grown to half the size and had half the flowers.

Here is your chance to find out for yourself. It is called double digging, and it is arduous. I'm not asking for full commitment here. Just do one small part of your new small garden.

Remove the top layer of soil one spade deep. Thats at least ten inches, and more is better. Set it aside. Then work up the next level of soil, adding all the organic material you can muster. Pine bark mulch is easiest, but leaves are great, too, if you use enough of them. Then put back the first layer and add organic matter and fertilizer to that.

Classicists will tell me that I am wrong, and I am. That is not the procedure you would use to double dig a larger plot, but it works for a small space, and that's what you have. A small and attainable project. Once you see how well plants grow there as opposed to right next to them where the soil has been only normally worked, you will want to double dig everything.

Now you can watch that spot for the rest of the summer and fall. And you will. But while you are staring, be thinking about something more interesting or elegant than petunias or impatiens. This fall you can put a little more effort into the soil and be ready for a great garden next spring.

Oh, and plant some bulbs in fall. Remember how good those petunias looked out the window all summer. Think how much more welcome crocus and daffodils will be next March.

Here's a thought. Get a packet of red lettuce seeds and scatter them along the edge. It will give a brand new garden a finished look effortlessly, and you can eat the lettuce. Even if you fail my new garden test, sprinkle some lettuce seeds in the bare spots in your existing garden now.

Maybe you are one of the rare people who don't have a window that cries out for a view. But you certainly have some place. Right at the end of the driveway to welcome you home? At the corner of the front walk? A small inside corner where the garage comes off the house? Or maybe an existing garden that could be a foot or two deeper or wider?

The point is that there are thousands of unwanted flowers looking for a home. You can make them happy and save a bunch of money and have a new garden. There is no down side. If you put this aside, determined to do it as soon as you have time, you need to face reality. Stop deluding yourself and hire someone to do your gardening.

Painted Ladies

I live in a town full of painted ladies, and I love it. Who wouldn't. As in most such towns, they congregate on one particular street.

In this and similar towns the founding gentry gathered in one neighborhood and in the last half of the last century build grand houses in a series of styles that have since become known collectively as Victorian, after the British queen who was shaped like a large house.

These were all painted white when I was growing up, which would have looked very strange to the original owners. About a decade ago one brave soul, in need of a paint job, bucked seventy years of spurious tradition and adorned a house in its original harlequin glory. Others followed. Painted ladies.

For some reason the enthusiasm for authentic restoration runs out of steam at the big brass handle on the front door. People who have put five figures into a paint job and mind-boggling amounts to make interiors just so go on to finish off the yard as if they lived in a 1970s raised ranch.

There are reasons for this, and there are excuses. Sometimes they blur. But let's be blunt: The real reason is that most people have no idea what Victorian yards looked like and don't bother to find out. Wainscoting is studied and reproduced to the most exacting detail, but outside the attitude is, hey, a tree is a tree and a shrub is a shrub.

Earlier houses were easier. Town houses from the 18th and early 19th centuries were built right on the street. Open the front door and you were on the sidewalk. That was because landscaping hadn't been invented yet, so there was nothing to put between the house and the street.

Colonial and Federal period burghers had no yard chores to do on Saturdays, which was a shame because there was no football and no TV to watch it on. Then about the time Victoria was crowned [the theme from *Jaws* fades in] the lawnmower was invented.

Men bought them—even back then guys were still guys and had to have any new tool that came along—and ran them up and down the sidewalk in front of their houses. It wasn't very satisfying, so new houses were built with yards, and landscaping commenced.

The revolution of 19th Century landscape design was at the same time subtle and profound. While earlier gardens at grand houses had been entities in themselves, the new American style had one overriding purpose: to enhance the house.

Victorians displayed their houses and framed them in the landscape. It stood proud, like a pimple on prom night. Large trees and shrubs gave context but did not hide the house. The lawn, not a foundation planting, created the base, and flowers and shrubs led the eye to the house.

Vistas seen from inside were every bit as important as the outside view. Landscape plans from the time show groves and pergolas and gazebos and parterres always with sight lines drawn in from important windows.

The basic concept was to integrate the house with Nature, but in the words of the time it was "nature adorned." The yard was supposed to look like God would have made it if God had been able to afford a top landscape architect.

The total effect was park-like rather than yard-like. In fact Central Park, designed by Frederick Law Olmstead in the 1850s, was a masterpiece of Victorian landscaping, though that is little appreciated by the muggers and winos today. Trees and shrubs are carefully placed to look as if they are not carefully placed. Ample use is made of groundcovers and vines.

On the town lot scale this concept was preached in *A Treatise on the Theory and Practice of Landscape Gardening, Adapted to North America; with a view to*...well, it goes on...by A. J. Downing in 1841 followed by several revised editions. It became the Bible of the new trend. For those obsessed with authenticity, the book has been reprinted by Dover Press under the more manageable title of *Landscape Gardening and Rural Architecture.*

In creating an imitation of nature, remember that trees and shrubs seldom grow in straight lines. In a Victorian landscape trees are planted at a distance from the house to form a backdrop to closer plantings. Shrubs are arranged in groups with different heights and textures, always keeping the view from inside in mind. The overall look is lush. Some might say overgrown.

Flower beds were bold masses of color, also visible from inside. That precludes the modern practice of planting flowers around the foundation of the house. Instead the beds are out some distance. The foundation is naked

A true parterre, a formal looking island bed of massed flowers, would be difficult for the casual gardener today. But in approximating an early Victorian bedding scheme remember that a quantity of a single kind of flower is preferred to a mixture of colors and types. Late in the period the writing of Gertrude Jekyll exerted its influence, so a turn-of-the-century house might have what has become known as the classic mixed border, but always away from the house.

If renovation enthusiasts know a smidgen about historically accurate landscaping, they fixate on the difficulties. The well-off of that era had cheap help, and lots of it, which we don't have today. And plant varieties in their century-old unimproved form are subject to every disease the Lord ever created. So, the reasoning goes, an authentic Victorian landscape would be prohibitively expensive to maintain in 21st Century America.

Horsefeathers. You no more need to create a duplicate of the yard that existed in 1870 than you need to duplicate the kitchen that came with the house. Like the new kitchen, you strive to create the feel of the period, but with up-to-date appliances to cut down on the labor. It is the age-old debate between restoration and evocation, and I come down solidly on the side of evocation. You want it to look right for the house without putting yourself in jeopardy of an INS raid.

A good approximation can be done using modern varieties of old standards. But most dedicated restorers, who can tell you every detail of hundred-year old wallpaper patterns, don't know where to start with the landscape. Your local nurseryman probably doesn't know much more than that he paid a dollar for that geranium and sells it for five.

You're going to have to research and learn. Sorry. You might try the Downing book or, more recently, *The New Traditional Garden* by Michael Weishan. Either that or plant clipped yews at the foundation and a grafted weeping cherry out front and hope no one notices the anachronism. They won't.

Conditioned Response

My delphiniums, normally seven to eight feet tall, topped out at three feet this year. I suspect our long, cool spring is the culprit.

That same long, cool spring gave me Chinese cabbage in June. Most years my spring sown crop bolts. But I always try it anyway, just in case we get exactly the right weather. Chinese cabbage is as fussy as Goldilocks. It like the weather just right. If it gets too hot, they bolt; if it gets too cold, they bolt.

If you've hung around gardeners as much as I have over the years, a pathology for which I am getting treatment, unfortunately group sessions with other gardeners, you have heard snippets like, "Been a bad

year for potatoes," or "Good year for corn." A few years back, hard as this is to believe, we had a bad year for cucumbers and some people actually cared.

As a gardener with too many years of experience, people expect me to have not only answers but solutions. Sometimes, though, there is neither.

Not always. A woman called me once about an orange tree she had brought back from Florida. An astute observer, she thought it was dead, and she wanted to know why. I went through the usual questions about signs of disease or insects, light, water. Finally I asked her what kind of pot it's in. Pot? She'd planted it in the back yard. Last fall. This woman had a weather-related problem.

More common are questions about peppers. Why aren't my peppers setting fruit?

Peppers are the opposite of Chinese cabbage. If it gets too hot or too cold, Chinese cabbage tries to set seed. If it gets too hot or too cold, peppers get cranky and refuse to set seed (i.e., fruit). The reason is obvious. We WANT peppers to do it, and we don't want Chinese cabbage to. Anyone who has gardened for more than a couple of seasons knows that the garden is a malevolent creature intent on driving us mad.

The next question that comes is, "What can I do to make my peppers set fruit." And the answer is nothing. Wait. The weather will change.

Tomatoes set fruit more readily. They wait until the end of the season to conspire with the weather to confound us. A cool summer will keep them sitting on the vine, green as emeralds, until September, when the ripening process races like a tortoise against the impending frost.

There are a couple of things you can do to nudge them along. The typical method is to visit the garden a couple of times a day and scream, "Turn, damn you, turn!"

Less emotionally satisfying but marginally more effective is root pruning. When you can't stand it any more, shove a spade or trowel into the soil, making a circle about a foot out from the stem, severing the roots. The tomatoes will get the message that you are unhappy with them and might ripen a few for you.

Rain is a weather condition we can take some minimal control over, at least if there is too little of it. We can water. Maybe you don't want to water your whole garden, but you might consider spot treatment for the most needy.

Onions, for instance, want a whole lot of water right about now, when they are forming their bulbs. Schlepping the hose out there every couple of days can pay big dividends.

For the most part, though, there is little we can do about the weather except understand it, learn to live with it, and of course, talk about it. Going out with a watering can won't do it. At best a watering can will wet the top quarter inch of the soil. If that. Better to water every few days than to sprinkle daily. In fact, better not to water at all than to sprinkle.

Iris

I like iris. I don't LOVE iris, but I like them. They are a sensuous flower that draws you in for a close look, at least in June.

I have a friend who has two or three thousand of them in his large and meticulously maintained yard. Three thousand iris and one hosta. I went over there in early June when they were at their peak to look around. It was a spectacular, if short lived, sight.

I don't have acres of iris. I have maybe a dozen kinds, a small patch of each, not a purple one in the bunch. If I want to see purple iris, I can take a short walk through the neighborhood and see all I want. In my garden are red iris and golden and bronze and mahogany and coral.

Those purple things in every yard are called German iris or tall bearded iris. There is also a dwarf form that is better in many ways. It has smaller, shorter flowers, but they form a solid blanket

of color; their big cousins don't do that. And they bloom a couple of weeks earlier than the big ones, which extends the bloom time of a depressingly brief display. The dwarfs also multiply prolifically.

Dwarf iris are particularly good for patio or deck tubs. For one thing, they are hardy as rocks, even in containers left outside over the winter as long as they don't get soggy. And the leaves are short, so it is easy to overplant them with annuals to hide them after the blooms fade.

Japanese iris have huge, spectacular flowers and slender leaves, and they bloom later than German iris, extending the season a bit further. You can plant them in the garden or grow them in a small pool or tub. They love water. I once had some escape into the roadside drainage ditch and try to take over the county.

The Higo variety of Japanese iris was specifically bred for pot culture, so they can be grown outside and brought into the house just as they bloom. The Japanese have an elaborate ceremony for Bringing In the Iris, a cross between the tea ceremony and the Alpine Bringing Down the Cows, which is a little less aesthetic. They all sit there in the living room for three days watching the flower open, which is why there are fewer Toyotas made in late June than at other times. When the bloom is gone, they move it back outside, no ceremony this time, so the frowzy foliage is out of sight.

And therein lies the problem with garden iris. They are gorgeous for a week or ten days and then pretty much pfthbthbthththff for the rest of the year. Worse than pfthbthbthththff; they're downright ugly. That's why I grow my iris in isolated groups surrounded by other plants so you can ignore what's left of the iris.

Grandma always would cut the leaf fans back by half after they bloomed. She thought they required that, but they don't. It's just to make them less visible, which is not necessarily a bad thing. It does, though, remove photosynthesizing green leaf surface, which slows their spread, which is also not necessarily a bad thing. If you want them to multiply, don't cut back the leaves.

The other problem with iris is the grass and weeds that grow up in the clump and cling to the rhizomes like a two year old to Mommy. My friend doesn't have this problem, but then he is single-handedly responsible for the shortage of cedar mulch on the east coast.

I don't know whether he is very lucky or very alert. Generally iris don't like a thick mulch. It can hold in moisture around the rhizomes and promote rot. In stony, well drained soil maybe you can get away with it. In soggy clay it is certain death.

The traditional method of ridding an iris patch of weeds is to pull the tops off and then go back a week later and pull the tops off again. My way is better. It's more work at first, but it lasts longer.

But first let me disabuse you of the common idea that perennials are flowers that you plant once and forget. (I can see perennial gardeners smiling.) Perennials actually take more work and certainly more savvy than the annuals that fill the megamart parking lots in May.

Unlike annuals, which bloom from the time you buy them until they die with the first frost, perennials usually bloom for only a few weeks. That means you have to carefully plan and plant different perennials to have a long season of color. You have to feed them and weed them and stake them and deadhead them and ...and...and well, they can be a lot of work.

They also need to be divided periodically, every three years or so with iris. And now is the time to do that, shortly after they bloom.

It's really easy. First do what Grandma did—cut the fan of leaves down by half. While she did it for no particular purpose except tradition, you do it now to cut down on transpiration. Leaves give off moisture. When you dig up a plant, you damage the roots, so they are limited in the amount of moisture they can replace. Cutting back the leaves can make the difference between survival and horticide.

With the leaves cut back, it is simple. Best of all, it happens in July when the most onerous garden projects are done. Lift the clump on a spading fork and drop it from waist high. That should knock off most of the soil. Break the rhizomes apart so you have pieces with three or four fans. Throw out the fusty bits.

Pull out all the weed roots from underneath. The grassy weeds will have stringy white roots that are easy to identify. Get them all, because a molecule of grass root will infest the whole replanted plot by next week.

It is needless to say, but I'll say it anyway. While the iris are out of the ground, take a moment to improve the soil where you will be replanting them. Iris like rich, well drained soil, though they will grudgingly tolerate almost anything. Dig in a thick layer of pine bark mulch and a handful of common garden fertilizer, and dig it deep. Do this often enough in every place where you divide a perennial and you will eventually end up with great garden soil without the burden of laboriously doing the whole border at once.

rhizome

Now replant the best iris rhizomes. If you plant them six inches apart, you'll have a full stand faster and need to divide them again sooner. Planted a foot apart, they'll still give you many nice flowers next year and it will be longer before you have to separate them again.

Normally, and with other perennials, I would argue for the wider spacing. But with iris there are reasons for closer planting. One, it isn't an onerous task to divide them in July, even every July, and two, the weeds will come back, sooner rather than later. And the best way to get the weeds out is to lift the patch. Even if they don't need to be divided, the easiest way to weed them is to lift them.

When you replant iris, make sure the top of the rhizome is right at the soil surface. People who complain that their iris don't bloom usually have them planted too deep.

Although irises are far from first in my heart, I admit that I miss them when they've gone.

Chartreuse

I am coming to terms with chartreuse. It's like a pain that you learn to live with. In fact, that's an apt analogy, because chartreuse is the color of a migraine.

The first chink in my chartreuse armor arrived years ago, and it wasn't my fault. It was a bonus plant a nursery stuck in with my order without my permission, a small hosta called, I think, 'Little Aurora'. I'm not sure, because after a decade the tag crumbled, but I still haven't been able to kill the plant.

I stuck it around the corner, about twenty feet down a shaded hedgerow. I chose that spot because I don't go down there very often. But every time I looked around that corner, there it was in the distance, glowing in the shade like a ray of sunlight piercing through the canopy.

I almost liked that look. So when I saw an ivy, unnamed and in a grocery store of all places, I decided to give it a try. There was only a tinge of the offending color around the edges mitigated by an apple green center. It looked almost nice near the hosta.

Next, as if to taunt me, Tesselaar sent me a new astilbe called 'ColorFlash Lime' in a more subtle shade of chartreuse (if that isn't an oxymoron) with feathery pink flowers. Despite myself, I liked it. It went into the hedgerow.

Then I got hooked on ornamental sweet potatoes. No garden should be without them, especially container gardens. The old standard is 'Blackie', but 'Sweet Caroline' is just as good, perhaps better for pots, and 'Sweet Caroline Bronze' is stunning. My sweet potato adventure could not be complete without 'Margarita', an eye-searing chartreuse. Unfortunately sweet potatoes hate shade, so I got to look at this hue in the sun. Grown intertwined with darker plants it wasn't as bad as I expected.

Now there is even a chartreuse sedum called 'Angelina'. They had big pots of it at a plant sale this spring. My good sense prevailed, and I was headed out the door empty handed when the announce-

ment came: Sedum now half price. It was like calling out, "Free beer." I left skid marks.

'Angelina' is an evergreen, or ever-chartreuse, ground cover sedum, much like 'Blue Spruce' except it isn't blue. Once home I realized I had no idea where to put it. Chartreuse is a hard color to place.

Fortunately with spreading sedums you have the option of trying them in several different locations at once and observing them in the best possible way, which is—gradually. Pick off several four-inch stems and stick the ends, two or three at a time, under a rock or brick or pot in different places. It will root and slowly grow, unobtrusive at first. As it gets big enough to notice, you can decide whether you want it there.

These have all been small plants, and like small pains, easy to bear. But now I find myself in possession of a new chartreuse Kolkwitzia, the beauty bush, called 'Dream Catcher', one of the Proven Winner ColorChoice shrubs. It will grow to six feet. The tag says it "lends intense color to a dull landscape." I'll bet it does. I can see it, for instance, lightening the heavy load of a dark evergreen windbreak. It would shine there and draw your eye like a spotlight. And as a bonus, the deer don't like the taste. I don't know what they think of the color.

I don't have a dark evergreen windbreak. So this shrub will spend time in a large pot. I will move it here and there, watching it for a while, until I find just the right spot.

Chartreuse is a difficult color to use. Some plants play nicely with it. Some fight like ten year old siblings. It requires a deft touch, but I'm starting to appreciate it. Or maybe I'm just getting used to the pain.

Water Plants

Houttuynia cordata—which as near as I can figure out is pronounced how-too-in-ee-uh—is a wonderful plant, a beautiful plant It is sometimes called the chameleon plant, but so are a dozen other better behaved species, so look at the small print. Houttuynia has gorgeous leaves in green and red and yellow and is irresistible in a catalog photo or a nursery bench. Don't ever, I mean DON'T EVER plant this in your garden.

I did. Many years ago. I'm still trying to pull it out, dozens of yards from where I planted it. The roots dive to the center of the earth and come back up where you least want them.

On the other hand, this is a great plant in pots for a small LINED water garden, someplace where the roots cannot escape. There is a lesson to be learned from this.

The lesson is that many plants we think of as garden plants are quite happy in a water garden. More important, bought as garden plants they are a fraction of the price of plants sold in pond stores as aquatics.

How many of you are plagued with green water? Lots of hands up. Thought so. OK. how many have spent money on devices that kill the algae, including filters you have to clean out all too often? Yuck.

You don't need them. The problem is that you don't have enough plants. Fish or fertilizers release nitrogen into the water. Nitrogen and sunshine cause the green algae to thrive. Green water. But water plants suck up the nitrogen and shade the surface, and the water clears. No equipment, no messy chores.

Japanese iris are great nitrogen suckers. If you have some in the ground or can find them at a garden center (at a late season mark down), you can plant them in your water garden now. But they will need repotting.

The reason is that potting soil or well amended, good garden soil, the kind of soil I have been nagging you to create, is bad. It has humus, organic matter, and that's a good thing. Usually. But humus floats. Put a pot with good soil in your pool and the humus will work its way out and litter the water surface.

You need to repot them in plain old dirt. For a good gardener, that can be hard to find, certainly not in YOUR garden. Cheap bags sold as "topsoil"—not the pricey name brand stuff but the buck a bag product—is usually pure "dirt." Or you can steal a trowelful or two from a less committed neighbor's garden after the sun goes down.

Water garden books tell you to use pots without holes. Thats wrong, at least for ponds with liners. A regular plastic nursery container with holes in the bottom lets the roots wander out to get that excess nitrogen.

Canna lilies (which like so many "lilies" are not lilies at all) are fine pond plants. You can buy tubers in spring for three or four bucks. The same thing growing in a display pool in a pond store will cost you fifteen.

Unfortunately they are not as easy as iris to move mid-season. Fortunately they multiply. If you have cannas planted in a patio tub or in the ground, let the first frost kill the tops, dig, and store the tubers dry and cool. They're easier than dahlias. Next spring you'll have enough to put back in your patio tub and in the pond as well.

The huge leaves of green elephant ears, *Colocasia esculenta*, are good for large ponds but too big for my little lily puddle. But not the smaller black versions like imperial taro and 'Black Magic'. Once hard to find and very dear, they now show up on big box benches for five bucks. If you buy them as garden or container plants, that is. Triple that if you buy them as pond plants.

The quaintly named bloody dock (*Rumex* species), also grows happily in water. And so does water celery, whose name should be a tip off. The point is to get as many plants as cheaply as possible into that pond. Plastic water lilies don't count.

And say good-bye to green water.

Compost

For once the experts got it right. The classic three-bay system is the very best way to make compost

You've seen it on the television gardening shows and read about it in books. You build three open bays side by side by side, each a three foot cube with an open front, like pony stalls.

You pile dead plants in the first bay, and when it is full and the pile has started to shrink, you shovel it all from the first bay into the second. Then you fill the first bay again with new dead stuff. When the time comes again, you shovel all the material from the second bay into the third bay, shovel all the stuff from the first bay into the second bay, and start filling the first bay again. It gives you an intimate understanding of how much a cubic yard really is.

After a few weeks or months, depending on the season and the number of plants that die, you shovel finished compost from the third bay. Brown gold. The closest thing to magic you can do for your garden. Then you refill the third bay from the second, the second from the first, and go find more dead plants.

There is only one little flaw with the classic three bay composting system. No one actually does it. Oh sure, everyone intends to set one up some day, even soon, as soon as he gets some time. But the time never comes and the grass keeps growing and the leaves keep falling. Or maybe the bays get built, but that constant moving from one to two and from two to three and empty three and start all over again gets real old real fast.

Thats why I advocate a simpler system that works because of a secret the experts don't want you to know. I'll whisper so they don't find out I'm spilling it.

You don't have to make compost. Compost makes itself.

It's true. If you go out in the woods you don't find a three-bay composting system in every clearing, do you? No. Leaves fall on the ground and turn into compost. Eventually.

So I use the all natural, totally organic P&W system—Pile & Wait. I pile the stuff up and wait until it's compost. It takes a little longer, it doesn't get as hot, but it works. After a year or so, I have compost. It may not be the best system, but it is better than a classic three bay array that never gets built.

The one drawback of the P&W system is that you have to wait a year for your first compost. I know people who won't use P&W because of that, though they have waited five or ten compostless years intending to build a three bay system. Anyway, once your first season is over, your supply of compost is as steady as the guy sweating out his turning and tumbling and moving from bay to bay. As you use last season's compost production, next season's is piling up.

Just mounding up plant material works. I proved that with Mount Compost, which I shall tell you about shortly when I get to the Things Not To Do part. It works, but cobbling together some kind of frame makes it even easier. And it looks better, if you are concerned with the appearance of your compost pile.

You can buy a compost frame, but the store-bought models have two problems. They're too small and way too expensive. One model, touted as "Our Most Economical Compost System" by one catalog, costs forty bucks and holds a measly 22 cubic feet. Whoever cooked up that one sure didn't have a maple tree. One 70 dollar job called a "kitchen composter" is a plastic bucket that you bury in the yard by the back door. We used to call that a hole in the ground, and it used to be a lot cheaper.

And the touted tumbler barrels are hopelessly inadequate for anyone with more than a condo balcony.

For a fraction of the price, a roll of wire fencing twelve feet long by three feet high will give you 38 cubic feet. Or thereabouts. My tenth grade geometry is a little rusty. Make a circle, tie the ends together with twist ties or twine, and start filling it.

Even cheaper, find a pile of wooden skids behind some large store or factory. Ask their permission (which they'll gladly grant) and take four. Tie them together to form an open-topped cube. In a few years the wood will rot out but the skid mine will still be there.

If you have the urge to actually build something, or if hubby needs a project to get him out of your hair for an hour, here's a simple and very effective compost frame. Take some lumber that has been lying around waiting for a greater destiny. Pieces 2 x 2 inches work best, but 2 x 4's will do if you don't want to split them. Make a three-foot square, bracing the corners with plywood triangles. OK, now picture this. You have your square. Using three more pieces, turn it into two three-foot squares at right angles making half a cube. Got that? Good. Now do it again.

You now have two sections, each half a cube. It's a good idea to dig that half can of avocado green paint that's been in the basement since 1968 and slap some on to help it last longer. Line each section with chicken wire or turkey fencing, whatever is on sale. Using four screen door hooks and eyes, two each top and bottom, hook them together to make a cube. Now you get to fill it.

Compost snobs who write weighty screeds make it unnecessarily complex. It's not. But there are a couple of simple things you can do to help the process.

The gurus tell us to mix brown material (leaves) and green material (grass), like the sandwich menu in *The Odd Couple*. But you may notice this time of year that there is a lot more of the latter than the former. You don't want to pile up all grass, believe me. I save fall leaves in garbage bags to mix with it.

You probably didn't have the good sense to do that, at least not

last fall. You'll have to scrounge brown material. It's not hard. Look for leaves that stuck in the corners, or get a bale of straw or some sawdust or wood chips. Mix it in with your grass clippings so they don't get all yucky. This coming fall you know what you have to do.

When your frame is full, unhook the ends, pull it off, and set it up right beside your first pile, which will hold its nice square shape. Next spring that first pile will have shrunk to half its height, and though the outside still looks like uncomposted dead plants, inside is brown gold.

I like to sift my compost, but that is optional. I built a cheap frame with quarter inch hardware cloth, and I spend mindless hours running compost through it. I put the finished compost in garbage cans and periodically go out and run my fingers through it like Scrooge McDuck in his vault. But you can take it straight from the pile to the garden if you already have some mindless activity that you prefer.

There are things you should do and things you shouldn't. Do chop up larger pieces into smaller pieces. I put a pair of hedge clippers by my pile and take a few chops whenever I walk by. Don't waste your money on compost starter. Do keep the pile moderately moist but not soggy. Don't put Christmas trees in the pile.

The books don't tell you that. But a while back my first frame, unpainted, rotted out, and I just started piling stuff up until I could get around to building a new one. I threw the Christmas tree on top. Then the next year's Christmas tree. By the time I got my new frame built, I had Mount Compost. I had to carve steps into the side to get up and dump stuff. When I started dismantling it, the ghosts of Christmas past were a real pain.

So if you opt for the most simple method, piling stuff up, don't put the Christmas tree in there. Or you can make an effective but rudimentary frame cheaply and easily.

If you don't yet have a compost pile, you just ran out of excuses.

Spinning Plates

Back when I was still in a cradle, there was this guy on Ed Sullivan who spun plates. That's pretty much all he did, and he did it about once a month. He'd stick a dowel up in the air, balance a plate on it, and start it spinning. Then he'd do the same with a second and a third. Pretty easy so far. Well, easy for him. I couldn't do it.

By the time he got to the fourth, the first one would start to wobble, and he'd have to run back and give it a boost. Then he'd start yet another one, run back to the first ones to keep them up to speed, on to another new one, back and forth, until he had ten or so spinning at once. That was his livelihood.

I've been thinking about this guy a lot in the last three years. Building a garden is a lot like spinning plates. You do one piece of the project, then move on to another and another. After a time you look back at that first section and see that it needs weeding and pruning and mulching and a couple of plants aren't right and need to be changed. The closer you get to completion, if that word can ever be used with a garden, the less time you have for new work because you spend increasingly more time on maintaining what you've already done.

For three years now only I have known what the back yard would eventually look like. In fact, only I have believed it would look like anything at all. But now it is starting to come together; even my wife is pleased. I'm down to some of the hardscaping features that give it shape and form. Hardscaping is a landscaping term for things like fences and walks, and it's something sensible people do first.

A fence, basket weave with a lattice topper, has gone in to back up the sixty foot mixed border on the north. It is a job I contracted out. Generally I do things myself, but I know my limitations. The thought of setting up posts one day, then coming back the next and expecting the fence sections to actually fit between them boggles my mind, but there are people who can do just that. A second, smaller fence masks the utility area outside the back door. Utility is a euphemism for garbage.

A few days ago I painted, or actually stained it. White. But as much as I hate painting, the job must be done again. The white is just too prominent. When you look, you see the fence. What you should see are the flowers. So after days of painful deliberation, I've decided it will be repainted a pale gray. As soon as I work up the nerve to tackle that job again.

The walkways I intentionally saved for last. I needed a couple of years to find out where people went. No matter how right a path looks on paper, people will go where they go. We see examples of that every day, a walk beautifully laid out, and leading off from it is a worn trail, cutting a corner here, making a short cut there. So I drew approximations on my plan, but now I'm laying pavement where the paths have already been worn.

I love brick and I love flagstone, but my budget was blown on the fences. So now the driveway is filled with nine tons of crushed stone that I bought, bricks that I scrounged and salvaged, and broken pieces of flagstone that I got at a nearby quarry, two bucks for all you can load from their scrap pile. The bricks will line the walks and hold down the edges of the plastic underlayment. Gravel is dumped between the bricks, bucket by laborious bucket. And the flags are laid in the gravel like stepping stones. It really looks nice, almost as if I'd chosen the style for appearance, not just because it was the cheapest thing I could come up with.

So there's that nine tons of gravel to move, while our car sits on the street. But the new fence has highlighted some plant errors in the mixed border, and they have to be tended to. Plants growing into their places need training and feeding. And the weeds won't stop while I work on the walks. It's going to be a long summer of spinning plates.

Small Treasures

Some of my very favorite plants go unnoticed by visitors. They'll spot a twelve inch dahlia blossom off in the distance and walk right by some little jewels that I treasure.

Take semps—sempervivum, the live forever plant, or as most people call them, hens and chicks. In spring, when other gardeners are wallowing in their daffodils, I am entranced by my semps. It is their best time of year, glowing with colors that gardeners who grow the common green ones wouldn't believe. If they looked at them.

Today I've been working on my coping. No, not in a spiritual, New Age sense. Coping, as in the stones you put around the edge of an artificial pool to make it look natural, in an artificial way.

Most people place the stones and forget them. I am constantly fiddling. A couple of years ago, I stuck some semps into the corners and crevices in the coping stones.

Some of the coping semps are deep red. And I had this bag of smooth river stones I'd bought a while back because they were a bargain. I sorted out the red ones and tucked them in around the russet semps. They are perfect jewels in this perfect setting, but I'm the only one who notices this six- by six-inch display.

So I have these stones, anally sorted by color, and there is a pile of black ones. I tucked them into a corner of the coping, but they looked naked.

Leading away from the pool is my cheapskate's path—three feet wide, edged with scrounged bricks, filled in with crushed stone, with flat rocks dug out of my garden placed footsteps apart on top. If you didn't know me, you'd think it was a walkway with a look I was trying to achieve instead of a simple way to make a walkway for 50 cents a foot.

Along the edges of the bricks, planted in the gravel, are several tiny sedums which nobody notices. One is called *Sedum atlanticum,* a mat of bright, bright green with rosettes the size of pin heads.

A couple of years ago one of those pin heads fell unnoticed onto the top of a small pot of fenestraria, a succulent with transparent patches on its fleshy leaves. It grew there, making a strange double plant that looks like nothing in this world.

I figured that if it would grow there, it would grow in the little pile of black stones. so I scattered a few pieces there. The contrast is exquisite. Normally if you try to do intentionally what has happened before by accident, it won't work. But this did, and now I have another favorite few inches of garden that everyone else will miss.

Toward the end of that path is my Nittany Lion shrine, a three foot replica in pewter colored fiberglass, which always gets noticed by football fans.

Gardeners may notice that it sits in a bed of *Heuchera* 'Pewter Veil', whose mottled leaves perfectly pick up the color of the lion. Almost no one notices the *Viola* 'Sylettas' planted along the stone wall in front of the 'Pewter Veil'. The pea size leaves hugging the ground match the marbling of the heuchera.

My garden is also full of tsatskes—animals and elves and insects made of concrete or metal or various space age materials. Some people put such ornaments right in your face. I like to hide them.

A friend gave me a pair of ceramic hedgehogs, mother and child, which hide in a patch of gray artemesias with only their noses sticking out. No one knows they're there, but I glance over every time I pass.

I'll still plant the dinner plate dahlias for others. And to tell the truth, I enjoy them too. But there is a special spot in my gardener's heart for these small spaces that are mine alone.

Rules

Some people like rules, even insist on them. And some people like to think.

The bane or the blessing—depending on your view—of rules is that they simplify a more involved decision. Here's an illustration. It's three in the morning, you pull up to an intersection where you can see half a mile of empty road in all directions, and the light is red. Now, you know as well as I do that there is no good reason to sit there until it turns green, but you do, don't you. Don't you?

Since rules are intended for people who can't think very well in the first place, they need to be kept simple. Wait at red lights. If you make that rule sensible by saying wait at red lights unless it would be downright silly, you defeat the purpose of having a rule, which is removing the need to make knowledgeable decisions.

My radio co-host, Judi Segebarth (whom I call O.J.—Other Judi —since my wife is also Judi), is a rule-ridden person. I say something that is eminently sensible, and she fumbles furiously through her Little Red Book to come up with some rule less than ten words and no word over two syllables, to "prove" that I'm wrong.

A couple of weeks ago a woman suffered from cucumber wilt— well, SHE didn't, but her crop did—and wondered what to do. I told her to plant some more cucumber seeds.

Loose papers started blowing off my desk, and I looked over to see O.J. thumbing through pages so frantically that she was whipping up gale force winds. With a triumphant AHA! she finds a chart that says the last planting date for cukes is July 10th.

Simple. Decisive. Even right much of the time. But that rule assumes that all autumns are the same and frost will come on the date stated, and you and I know that they aren't and it won't.

I always plant vegetables later than the Garden Bishop allows. There is empty space late in the season, and you might as well do something with it. Most years the frost gets them, as the rule predicts, and I lose a nickel's worth of seed. But some years I have picked fresh beans for Thanksgiving dinner.

Last week we were talking about dahlias, the king of the late summer garden. Dahlias are not a subtle plant. You grow them for dazzling blossoms, the bigger the better. And to make them bigger and better, I fertilize in August and September using a fertilizer with a very high middle number, like 10-60-10.

Buds and blossoms need phosphorus; that's what that middle number is. Fertilizers with 60 percent phosphorus were very hard to find until the last couple of years. They were made only by specialists, and only the biggest garden centers carried them. Now the garden departments of most megamarts carry some knock-off.

Well, no sooner had I said to fertilize dahlias now, while the buds were swelling, than my co-host threw another rule at me. No, she said, you should not fertilize after July, and she waved some book in my face to prove it.

This is a rule made for those who do not care to understand how fertilizers work. And it dates from a time when high phosphorus fertilizers were uncommon. If you give a normal balanced fertilizer to a perennial, shrub, or tree late in summer, the nitrogen will provoke new growth when the plant should be getting ready for winter dormancy.

But there is almost no nitrogen in the formula I was using on the dahlias. And besides, it is unlikely that they would winter kill in my basement, which is where I keep them. And annuals should get a dose of fertilizer, too. They aren't going to survive the winter anyway.

All this is too much to explain in a rule simple enough for those who don't want to bother themselves with thinking. But my readers are smarter than that. And for the few who aren't, here's a rule: Fertilize dahlias with a high phosphorus formula in August.

Prop Box

I can't believe I forgot. There are things I forget with great regularity, some I forget at random, others I forget on purpose. But I never, NEVER forget to take along Ziploc bags when I visit a garden.

Any garden you tour can contain treasure, a plant that is special, a plant you don't have, a plant that needs a bit of careful pruning or pinching. I am always happy to help, and the bags are to avoid littering the ground with the clippings. I can be very tidy when the occasion calls for it.

OK, I'm pinching plants. In public gardens this practice causes a condition called finger blight. It is definitely not a good thing to pinch plants from a public garden. But few back-yard gardeners would deny a visitor a small piece of a prospering plant. That is why I always do the right thing and ask permission from anyone who could be watching.

Given reasonable conditions, plant parts will survive several hours, some for several days, in a closed bag. Plants that have fragile leaves and stems, impatiens for instance, benefit from baptism. Splashing a few drops of water on the leaves will help keep them fresh.

Use common sense in tucking the bag away. Put it under the front seat rather than on the back window shelf. If you happen to have a cooler in the car, perfect.

149

Once home, slips switch sects and go in for full immersion baptism. Soak the entire cutting in water for an hour.

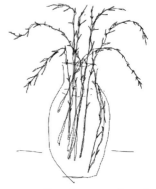

Now listen carefully. I am about to reveal one of the most closely guarded secrets of the hermetic branch of the gardening community—willow water.

Willows are a remarkable family of trees and shrubs, from the early bloom-ing pussy willow to the giant weeping willow. Very fast growing and flexible, the branches are used in basket weav-ing. Perhaps most important, people have known for thousands of years that willow relieves pain. Compounds found in willows are similar to aspirin, and animals in distress will eat it with gusto.

For the gardener, willows have another magical property. You know that if you cut a stem off a willow and stick it in moist ground, it will root overnight. That is because it is full of hormones that promote rooting, and that is the secret of willow water. If you cut a dozen slim willow branches and soak them overnight, leaves and all, in a couple quarts of water, you will have a solution that will turn your brown thumb green faster than a five dollar watch. Anything soaked in this water will take up the hormones and root faster. I also use willow water to wet the medium in prop boxes and pots. I hate it when I find an old wives' tale that works, but this one does.

If you have just a couple of cuttings, you can root them in four inch pots filled with a mixture of half peat-based potting soil and half Perlite, both available in any garden department. There is a right way of doing this and at least a dozen wrong ways. Here is the right way.

First, no matter how much it hurts, pinch off all flowers and buds. A plant facing the prospect of imminent death will do whatever it can to extend its line. If there is a flower, it will try to set seed. You want it to put all its effort into growing roots.

Take a tip cutting four to six inches long. If it is a plant with large leaves, trim half of each leaf off. Pinch the bottom couple of leaves off and stick the still wet stem up to the remaining leaves in some rooting powder. Willow water is great, but willow water and rooting powder together are super. Make a hole in the medium with your finger, stick the cutting in and lightly firm the mix around the stem.

 Enclose the pot in a bread bag with the open end tucked under the pot and keep it in a bright spot, but no direct sun. In as little as a week with some plants, a few weeks for others, a root ball will form. When you tug lightly on the cutting and it resists, it's time to pot it up in regular soil. Congratulations, you're a father. Or a mother.

That's retail propagation. But there is a better way. I do it wholesale. I am constantly rooting cuttings, not just those pinched from strangers, but my own. I do it for a number of reasons, a compulsive neurosis being only one of them.

Whenever I bring a new plant home, I make a copy of it as soon as I can. I give it to someone. That way, when I kill my plant, I'll know where to go for a replacement.

When I want multiples of some special and expensive plant in spring—geraniums or New Guinea impatiens or fuchsia—I have two choices. I can buy several, or I can buy one and make cuttings. Guess what I usually do.

Even when I don't need extras, I root cuttings. Many plants need pinching back to grow well, and there is no sense throwing the pieces out when you can turn them into new plants. I give them away to soften up people from whom I may one day want to bum a plant they have.

Given my profligate cloning practices, the indoor plant space gets crowded in winter. So instead of bringing in a big pot, I take a cutting. By spring it will grow into a plant large enough to take more cuttings to put outside.

In the spirit of full disclosure, I must admit that this does not work all the time. For example, it doesn't work very well with annuals, plants that grow from seed, flower, set seed and die, all in one season.

Many of the plants we grow as annuals, though, are perennials in their native tropics. If we do not abandon them to a cruel, cold death in October, they can live on for years. Marigolds and zinnias will die, no matter what you do, but begonias, geraniums, coleus and many, many more can be nearly immortal with a little help.

How can you tell the difference? Well, you can look it up in a good gardening book. Or you can try a cutting and see if it takes.

For the number of cuttings I do I use a clear plastic sweater box with a clear lid, once common, now increasingly hard to find. No matter. Any sweater box with a pane of plastic or glass on top, even kitchen plastic wrap, will do. In the bottom goes a two inch layer of rooting mix. It sits in the shade on my potting bench. Beside it is my jar of rooting powder and crock of willow water.

Any time I have a sprig in my hand, it takes less than a minute to dip it in the powder and stick it in the box. Usually I need to take something out to make room, but there is usually something ready to come out and be potted up. In winter this setup moves inside and keeps pumping out plants.

For someone who wants a cutting or two, the four inch pot and bread bag system works. But for the truly obsessed, you need a prop box and a supply of Ziploc bags.

Bill

Bill walked in about eight years ago. He marched over to the food dishes, ate his fill, threw up and fell asleep.

The last thing we needed was another pet. We already had a dog, two cats, a parrot, and miscellaneous smaller birds and beasts. But it's not as if we were asked.

152

The cat that moved into our house that day would have been thrown out of any respectable barn. Or alley, for that matter. Well past his prime—if he ever had a prime—he was nothing but skin and bones and appetite. His coat was appalling; mange comes to mind, but that is somehow inadequate. Chronic tooth problems gave him breath that could strip paint, and on those rare occasions when he washed himself, that stench permeated his whole body, indeed the whole room, and the white patches of fur turned brown. He drooled unremittingly, and his hobby was barfing.

Why keep such a cat? We really weren't consulted. The other animals, normally fiercely territorial, welcomed him instantly as part of the family. Besides, we quickly discovered a purr that could rattle the dishes in the cupboard and a sense of...well, humanity. Strong as a lion, he was nonetheless gentle as a lamb: When he decided to leave your lap, he left, no power could hold him, but there was never a scratch left behind.

Bill became my garden cat. As I stooped over a bed, I would prepare myself for the thump as he landed gracelessly on my back, where he would stretch out and languorously rest a damp chin on my shoulder, watching to make sure I did everything to his satisfaction. After I had thrown him off five or six times, he might grudgingly retreat to a ladder that hung horizontally on the side of the garage, where he would continue his observation, lanky legs stretched out fore and aft and belly spilling over the ladder rail. Unrestricted by my shoulder, the ever-present string of drool would elongate to several inches, swinging in the breeze, sometimes catching the sun in tiny rainbows. What a cat.

Supervision was his forte, but he was not above lending a paw where he saw the need. I never got seeds planted to suit him, for example, so he had to rearrange any newly planted bed. And he took a special interest in fertilization. All cats love the loose,

freshly spaded soil of a seed bed, and commercial repellents won't even slow down a determined cat with a mission.

So for many years my first assignment every morning was a walk through the garden, a cup of coffee in one hand, a small shovel with a very long handle in the other. Eventually I found a partial solution.

Over the years I had accumulated small scraps of hardware cloth, chicken wire, and miscellaneous fencing—the sort of thing normal people would throw out. Tossing pieces on the soil surface where seeds were planted prevented the cats from scratching, and they lost interest. As soon as the seedlings show, it seems less enticing, and the cover comes off. It's not perfect, but it helps.

Bill didn't resent these measures, just as I never resented his peculiar ministrations. Those of us who love living things, plant and animal alike, have learned what compromise really means.

Years after discovering this trick, I still make my morning walk. It's become a habit. And the truth is that I'm not a very methodical person, so the protective cover is sometimes forgotten, and the news quickly goes out to every cat in the neighborhood. But the real reason is that, except for brief moments that are less than inspiring, it is a pleasant routine. I have the opportunity to greet each plant on a daily basis, inquire of its health, enjoy the garden for a while with a cup of coffee in my hand instead of a hoe.

For many years Bill joined me every morning, strolling at my feet —drooling and belching, purring and coughing—but no longer.

Bill died last week. He went softly, with the dignity that was so surprisingly a part of him. Oh, we've lost pets before, and we will again, and it always hurts. But this elderly stray was indefinably special. He slept with my daughter, watched TV with my wife, but he was my buddy, my garden cat, and I'll miss him.

That night we talked about the empty spot in our lives and decided there would be no rush to fill it. We had our Princess, an

elegant dowager of sixteen plus years, who no longer adapted well to changes in the family composition, and she deserved our concentrated attention in her remaining time. I would learn to work alone. Besides, how could a cat like Bill be replaced.

Five days after I had buried Bill under the lilac where he liked to sleep on hot afternoons, I was sitting cross-legged in the middle of the lawn contemplating thatch. From nowhere a tiny, orange striped ball of fur and energy came racing. He jumped on my lap and started purring. Our inquiries provided not a hint of his provenance, but I think his orders came from under a lilac, issued by a spirit who knew I needed help in the garden. We named him Rufus, but after a couple of days his vitality earned him a sobriquet: The Kitten From Hell. Nothing that moved was safe. We loved him instantly.

Rufus doesn't drool or belch or choke, and he isn't much of a garden cat, not yet. He's too young to take his responsibility seriously. But he's learning. I have no doubt that as his youthful exuberance abates, my garden will benefit greatly from his stewardship. He sleeps with my daughter and watches TV with my wife. And the beat goes on.

There are those who resent cats in their garden, I know. As a newspaper columnist, the most frequent question I get is how to keep them out. But these people love their garden too much, and they miss a larger vision of love. If a genie appeared and offered me three wishes for the gardeners of the world, those wishes would be for a prosperous garden, a fine cat to share it with, and a good shovel with a very long handle.

Datura and Brugmansia

Linnaeus was the first taxonomist. He devised the binomial system and classified all the plants he knew into genus and species.

You may think those botanical. names are complicated, but it was really a simplification. For example, *Aceris fructu herba anomala flore tetrapetalo albo* became *Begonia acutifolia.* A lot easier to fit into the small lines of an order form.

I don't know who the second taxonomist was, but I am certain of one thing: The minute he came along, he and Linnaeus started to argue, and their successors have been arguing ever since.

Like Republicans and Democrats, taxonomists are divided into two warring parties—the splitters and the clumpers. The reason is that plants don't fall neatly into boxes with solid lines around them. They exist on a continuum, each a tiny bit different from the last and the next, and taxonomists get to superimpose the boxes. The clumpers draw a few big boxes, the splitters many tiny ones.

Take brugmansia and datura. They used to be in one big box -- datura. Some had large trumpet flowers hanging down, others similar trumpet flowers pointing up. The splitters said they were two different genera; the clumpers insisted they were all the same genus but some took Viagra. Since Viagra hadn't been invented at that time, the splitters won, so now there are two boxes.

I grow several varieties of both, and I've noticed differences. Not only is their appearance different beyond the recumbence or verticality of the flowers, but they are handled differently.

This year for the first time I an growing the common white datura, *Datura stramonium.* I say "common" only because it is an American native, jimsonweed, but there is nothing common about its beauty.

Jimsonweed produces many large, pure white trumpets above handsome smoky green foliage. The blooms last only briefly, but there are always more coming on.

Another datura, *Datura metel*, I have grown for a couple of decades. In fact, I had a hand in introducing it into commerce. The trumpets are double, a tube within a tube, white inside and rich purple outside, with a ruffled edge. A stunning flower.

These are both annuals that die at the end of the season, but it is easy to save the seeds and start them over in early spring. Start them just like tomatoes.

Brugmansias are a little more trouble and a lot more impact. They're perennials, so they can live for years, getting bigger and better each year. Many deck and patio gardeners buy one at the beginning of the season and abandon it in fall, getting a new one the next year. They will never see the full glory of a two or three year old plant, a six-foot shrub with fifty blooms open at one time.

Since you start daturas fresh each spring, you can plant them in the ground. But to save brugmansias over the winter, they should be in large containers. I've seen television hosts dig up brugmansias, put them in a garbage bag, and claim they'll overwinter that way. Personally I think they throw it out once the cameras stop and put a new one in the bag for the spring show.

If you have a big south window, you can bring it in and treat it like a gigundous house plant. It'll drop some leaves, but they're big and easy to pick up. If you have the window but not the space, you can cut it back to 12-inch stubs; it will resprout in a more manageable size.

I don't have enough windows for all my brugmansias, so I let the first frost scare them into dormancy, cut them back, and stuff them in a cool basement.

So I suppose there is a difference. But I don't care about the boxes taxonomists draw. I just care about the big, beautiful, sweet scented flowers.

SEPTEMBER

Garden Aerobics

I was wakened at 6:00 am this morning by the thump, thump, thump of aerobics in the next room. After an hour of house-shaking activity I gave up, got up, and found a glorious late summer day, sunny and mild. The golf course near our home is infested with people in funny clothes. Joggers swarm the river bank. My wife and daughter are now off on a lengthy power walk. Everyone is demented.

I do not exercise, and I do not understand people who do. That is not to say I don't move, even perspire occasionally. After all, it's tough to garden without leaving your easy chair, though there are some garden writers in New York City who manage. Suffering occasional exertion is necessary. But I don't exercise for the sake of exercise.

Imagine my surprise, then, when I learned that what I am doing is at least as healthy as running every day or subjecting myself to Nordic skiing in my bedroom. Maybe even healthier. And at the end I get tomatoes and roses. A runner only gets home.

Gardening simulates a lot of familiar exercises. You have your knee bends and that bending over at the waist thing. A thirty dollar spade can give you as good an upper body workout as a thousand dollar Whatchamacallit Turbo 5000. And if you've never been able to work up a lot of enthusiasm for double digging garden beds for horticultural reasons, you might consider it as part of your fitness regimen.

Aside from fine exercise, gardening nourishes both body and soul. Exertion in the vegetable garden ultimately yields healthy food. I know you can jog to the supermarket and get healthy food, but

when you grow it yourself, you'll actually eat it. There is no potato chip rack in your garden. And to reduce stress levels, what better than contemplating a bed of flowers.

My approach to exercise makes great good sense. But good sense is never enough for true believers. They must have their activity sanctioned by a guru who has written about it and provided a Program to follow. I don't count.

If that is what you must have, just Google "exercise" and "gardening" and you will be presented with millions of pages of instructions and advice, blogs and tweets, and more than a few books. They will show you many ways to turn common garden chores into a strenuous full body work out. That is for people who don't think gardening isn't already work enough, if there are any such people. (And I suppose there are; otherwise Jane Fonda wouldn't be rich.) For the rest of us, there is common sense information on how to get the most out of our routine. And since a lot of exercise freaks don't know diddlysquat about growing things, you can even find advice on gardening.

But enough of this. I'm exhausted just thinking about it. I Googled "puttering" and "gardening" and found a few pages more to my liking.

Geraniums

Geraniums are a cliché. Victorian parterres bedded with red blobs. I don't even know what a parterre is, but I think it's something like a fire escape, because I always see geraniums on fire escapes. Geraniums are as indestructible as the cast iron with which the Victorians ornamented their gardens. They laugh at summer heat and drought. Potted specimens dumped in a corner and forgotten for weeks still cling to life. Trimmed and watered, they soon return to bushy health.

160

They are uninteresting, common plants, beneath contempt for a serious gardener, and I can't imagine why I have so many. Well, yes I can. It's because I can't kill the damn things, and I can't bring myself to throw out a living plant. A begonia that catches my eye has the good grace to turn brown and fall over after a decent interval, making room for new plants. But every geranium I ever had I still have, clogging my sun porch in winter. I once even tried "forgetting" some, leaving them ignored outside until Thanksgiving. They didn't care.

Like an ugly dog, if they hang around long enough, you get grudgingly attached to them. I even have a favorite geranium, which is like having a favorite brand of pimento loaf. Close up, the geranium called 'Picasso' shimmers with fuchsia and orchid blushed with tangerine and a couple of colors that haven't been named yet, but from any distance it's just another red blob.

Another geranium that has some charm is 'Swiss Miss'. You know how it is when you walk through a nursery in spring—like grocery shopping when you're hungry. You'll pick up things you'd never buy in saner moments. So I got this two dollar plant with dark green, thumbnail sized leaves. By July it was hidden under a haze of fire engine red flowers, not the blobs of traditional plants, but open, almost lacy blossoms.

If geraniums are homely in summer, they are downright frowzy in winter. Leaves drop, stems stretch and get weak, flopping about here and there, looking more like a weedy vine than the compact plants of July. Many think this is due to low light levels in winter, and to be sure that doesn't help. But often too much warmth is more to blame than too little light. When days are short and dim, geraniums like it cool.

For this reason geraniums and unheated sun porches were made for each other. The cold temperatures keep the plants from getting too leggy, as they will in a warm living room, and there is probably no brighter spot in the house. Temperatures in the 40's at night rising into the low 60's during the day are ideal. It should stay above freezing, but if the temperature drops lower on some

frigid night, your geraniums probably will survive. They'll look terrible, but then they didn't look that good to begin with. And in the midst of winter, even a tawdry geranium blossom looks good.

If you want to be assured of winter blossoms, let your geranium grow strong outside during the summer, but pick off every flower bud as it forms. It's tedious, but when you bring it back inside in fall and stop pinching, it will be as eager as a teenager in love.

In March geraniums need to have the weak winter stems cut back to prepare for new summer growth. At least half the plant must be hacked away, and two thirds won't hurt it. You end up with a pile of plant pieces that will root in a week or so in damp sand or vermiculite. If you have never tried to root cuttings, geraniums are a good plant to learn on because they're so easy. So I end up with even more geraniums for bedding and an even worse space problem next fall.

Some people try the old Victorian method to keep geraniums over the winter, knocking the soil off the roots in fall, cutting the leaves off, and hanging them upside down from the basement rafters. But old Victorians had old Victorian basements—earthen floored, cool, dark, and damp, very different from the furnace room of a raised ranch. It may be hard to kill a geranium, but hanging them naked in a modern furnace room is one method that works.

The geraniums we know so well, those ubiquitous denizens of window boxes and Memorial Day pots, are called zonal geraniums because the markings on their leaves look like zones to those with an imaginative mind, but there are other kinds. When you walk into that big nursery next month and see acres of red lollipops, you might get lucky and find one small table hidden away in the back corner with something different.

As you head for that table, squeezing between the benches packed with the familiar plants, you'll probably bump your head on hanging baskets of cascading geraniums or ivy geraniums. It is tempting to take some home for the front porch, but remember that they are geraniums after all and want a lot of sun. If your porch roof shades them all day, they won't do well. On the other

162

hand, there is nothing better for a window box on the south side.

Back in the corner you may find some plants classed as fancy-leaved geraniums. They look like zonals on psychedelic drugs. One called 'Mrs. Cox' dazzled people over a hundred years ago with leaves splashed red and yellow. And another of the type, 'Vancouver Centennial', has maple-shaped leaves colored terra cotta and apple green. It is stunning in a clay pot.

You might also find on that out-of-the-way table some plants that are even more boring than the zonals and wonder why they bother selling them. They are scented geraniums. Rub a leaf and sniff.

A peppermint geranium has hung out in my plant room for two decades, abused and ignored, periodically cut back almost to pot level. The leaves are lightly felted, so soft that you just have to touch them, and when you do the scent of mint lingers on your fingers. Our dog occasionally brushes past; it even makes him smell good.

Other scented geraniums smell like apple (another favorite of mine), cinnamon, cloves, citrus, coconut, strawberry, or various evergreens. One is indistinguishable from Old Spice aftershave lotion. Most scented geraniums are small plants, ideal size for a windowsill. There are usually no flowers worth noting, but if you garden for more than one of the senses you should have scented geraniums.

Regal geraniums don't smell nice, but believe it or not, they're actually attractive, even beautiful. I know they are; I've seen pictures. But I can't grow them. Regal geraniums like cool summer weather, especially nights, and our summers don't always cooperate. Still their pansy-faced flowers often seduce me at the nursery, and I keep trying.

A spot that gets a few hours of morning sun followed by afternoon shade will keep them blooming until a mid-summer heat wave sets in. Sometimes I can keep them alive for a couple of years, but they don't have the tenacity of the zonals. It's nice in a way, though, to have a geranium that actually dies.

The best, and the hardest to find, of the less common geraniums are the miniatures. These tiny duplicates of familiar varieties grow only a few inches high with leaves the size of a nail head, the perfect windowsill plant. Other than size, they are identical to the big ones. Cute little things. They should be more widely sold, but you seldom see them in a nursery.

When you want something special, you go to a specialist. There are several on the Internet, some with hundreds of varieties. Do not insult these enthusiasts by trying to order some garish red flower you can get down the street.

Before long your house can be as full or red blobs and fancy leaves and sweet scents as mine is. And maybe it is a horrible waste of space, but if I ever find out what a parterre is, I'll be ready.

Fall Planting

I must confess. This summer's heat wave and drought were not a result of global warming. I caused it, and I am deeply sorry.

It was one of those things that seemed like a good idea at the time. A new garden I was building had a small circle of grass planned for the center, and I decided to plant it in late June. Yes, I know summer is the worst time to start a lawn, I should know better, but it was only ten feet across and within reach of the hose. I figured I could water every day.

Mother Nature saw me scatter the seed, smiled wickedly to herself, and jacked up the thermostat. Grass does not like hot weather, especially newly sprouted grass. Weeds do.

So it is time to plant my small lawn again. And that's fine, because fall is really the best time to start grass. The ground is still warm, the nights are turning cool—perfect conditions. A scattering of 5-10-5 garden fertilizer (NOT the normal, high nitrogen lawn food), another scattering of seed, and it will be up and growing, even cut once or twice before winter hits.

While many seasoned gardeners know that September is a great time to plant grass, few realize that they can also plant some vegetables. Normal gardeners plant their seeds in May and put the packets away. Better gardeners plant some seeds again in mid-July for a fall harvest. But the truly demented among us are going through our seed packets now for crops that can be planted in mid-September, carefully protected, and harvested first thing next spring. Forget tomatoes and peppers, but you have a good chance with spinach and lettuce, especially bibb and loose leaf lettuce.

You may think these are not hardy, and you are right. Sort of. The problem is that we try to process an analog world with a digital mind. Our brain says yes or no, on or off, hardy or not hardy. But some plants are a "maybe, just maybe." Some may survive a mild winter only to succumb to a normal one next season. A plant may live for years on one side of your house and die if moved around the corner. Some are half hardy, a little hardy, almost hardy, barely hardy, or marginally hardy.

Lettuce and spinach are in the "maybe" class. They'll take cold, just not quite as much as we have to offer them in January. But they have a good chance of making it given the right conditions, some winter protection, and a little luck. Overwintering them against their will is neither simple nor certain, but, when it works, eating from your own garden in April is the reward.

The easiest way is to use a cold frame if you have one. And if you don't, perhaps you can make a temporary frame. Bales of straw arranged in a rectangle and covered with plastic or a window sash left over from a remodeling job work fine. Next spring you can use the straw to mulch the vegetable garden. But I don't have a good spot for such a setup, and besides I never take my own advice.

In mid-September I plant my seed in a raised bed. You can plant in flat ground, but raised beds dry and warm earlier in spring, and early is what we're after. You can frame a bed with lumber, but it isn't necessary. Just rake soil from the paths into the row to make a flat-topped mound a foot or so wide and a few inches high.

Plant the seed thickly, and don't thin the seedlings. Winter will do that for you. You want seedlings two or three inches high before cold weather stops their growth. If cold comes early, cover the patch with floating row cover, that translucent white fabric you get in garden stores, or a plastic tunnel to extend the season.

When nights drop into the twenties, it's time to bundle up. The object is to insulate the seedlings from the bitter cold air and hold in the heat that radiates up from the ground. I use straw piled loosely ten to twelve inches deep and covered with floating row cover to keep it in place. Some use clear plastic tunnels. I once tried using those plastic packing peanuts, but after spending two years chasing them around the yard I never did that again. They might be better behaved in a cold frame.

Early next spring, as the sun strengthens, I remove the straw, leaving the floating row cover on. The salad fixin's in my raised bed are often on the table while other gardens are still too wet to be worked. All the work of fall is justified by that first bite.

In some years nature doesn't cooperate and in others I don't get my seedlings covered as soon as I should. But I have a fallback plan—January planting.

If you have ever let lettuce or spinach go to seed you will have noticed volunteer seedlings all over your garden. Weeds. The seed is winter hardy even if the plants aren't. So when that January thaw has me itching to get out in the garden and do something—a-nything!—I take a couple of packets of seed with me and scatter them on the cold, wet ground. When the spring sun warms them, they'll sprout and grow, not as early as the fall-planted seedlings but early enough. No January thaw? No problem. You can actually scatter seeds on the snow.

For some plants fall planting isn't just optional, it's required. Bulbs like tulips and daffodils are planted now so that they can grow roots over the winter and bloom in spring. But remember that garlic is also a bulb, and though some plant it in early spring, it really wants fall planting.

In a pinch you can plant garlic you buy in the grocery store. But that garlic probably came from Gilroy, in the central valley of California, and you may have noticed that our climate here is different from California's. Better to buy garlic for planting from a local grower, farmers' market, or garden center.

When you break the bulb apart into individual cloves, note which end is the pointy end and which end has the roots. The cloves should go in root down, about three inches deep and four inches apart. Garlic will reward you for improving the soil, digging in compost and bone meal. If you can't push the clove in three inches without a trowel, you need to work at it some more. Garlic can be planted as long as the soil is not frozen and harvested next July.

Some people plant the so-called elephant garlic, with mixed results. It is advertised as milder tasting, sissy garlic, but in fact it isn't garlic at all, and it is only marginally hardy here in Zone 5. If you must try it, use a heavy mulch.

Fall is also a great time to plant perennials, trees and shrubs. The plant can grow a strong root system and establish itself without the stress of summer heat and drought. And the weather is cool enough that you can put some real effort into soil improvement without fear of diaphoretic excess.

Fall-planted ornamentals don't want any general purpose garden fertilizer. Nitrogen could prod them to make new top growth, which you don't want this late in the season. But a good starter feeding with a high phosphorus formula like 10-60-10, often sold as a "bloom booster," is nice if you have it handy. Water the new plant in thoroughly and water weekly until the ground freezes.

A good mulch of ground bark, wood chips, or leaves five or six inches deep should be added when you plant. I know that the books say you shouldn't mulch ornamentals until the ground freezes, so perhaps a few words on the Tao of Mulch are in order.

Mulch keeps cold ground cold and warm ground warm. You mulch established plants late in the season, AFTER the ground freezes, to keep the ground frozen and avoid a freeze/thaw cycle in

spring that can break tender feeder roots. New plantings should be mulched now, though, to keep the ground from freezing too early and allow the new roots to grow. The soil will eventually freeze, and then the mulch will protect it from thawing.

The novice does most of these jobs in the spring and then sits back and relaxes. I am told that some proto-gardeners even go away for a vacation in the middle of prime gardening season. But the truly demented gardener, with proper planning, can find chores to keep him busy almost all year long.

Dahlias

My dahlias behaved strangely this season. They grew the way they were supposed to.

The package label on just about every dahlia I've ever bought says it grows to four feet. I don't think they really know; the marketing people just decided four feet was what would sell.

Mine commonly grow to twice that height. But not this season. The 'King of the Fall Garden' this year is only a prince. I have never understood the peculiar combination of sun and rain and temperature that makes some years great for some plants, other years terrible. Nevertheless, beset by a poor crop, I'll offer up the strange growing conditions of that season (and every season has SOMETHING strange) as an excuse. And when conditions are on the nose and the garden thrives, I credit my skill.

So the dahlias are not very good this year, but dahlias are like sex. Even when they're not very good, they're still great.

I have loved dahlias since we were newlyweds living in Germany. Every fall there was a Frau at the Saturday market in our village with three dozen cans of huge  dahlias on long stems that she sold for a dime each. A dollar's worth would make a massive bouquet, and they easily lasted until the next Saturday when we stocked up again.

Today I still think of dahlias mainly as cut flowers for fall. Though I do have a few small ones in my mixed border and in my container array, I grow most of them in the vegetable garden out behind the garage. That way when I cut all the best blossoms I don't feel as if I'm robbing my flower garden. The row where there once were cukes and squash is now a riot of color.

Dahlias are impressive flowers easy enough for the beginner. In late spring plant the tuber three or four inches deep in good soil and full sun. They'll take half day exposure, but they really like direct sun from dawn to dusk. The more sun, the more flowers.

Though they'll grow in common garden soil, a little effort pays off extravagantly. They love rich soil with lots of compost or bagged manure and a handful of granular 5-10-5. Then supplement it every few weeks with a liquid 15-30-15 fertilizer. The combination of organic fertilizers like compost along with chemical fertilizers will give you dramatically more vigorous plants, no matter what you're growing, than either alone.

There is a downside to this, of course. Huge plants heavy with bloom have a tendency to fall over in summer storms, so they're no longer six feet tall; they're six feet wide. Some gardeners stake them and tie them to the stakes every few days. I don't have the discipline for that. I use the same cages I use for tomatoes—not those flimsy things they sell for tomato supports, but sturdy five-foot tall cylinders made from concrete reinforcing wire.

In bountiful years sometimes even this isn't stout enough. I bought some 20-foot pieces of half inch concrete reinforcing rod—call it

rerod and the guy at the building supply will think you know what you're doing—under four bucks, and cut each with a hacksaw into four five-foot pieces. Pound one firmly into the ground next to each cage and wire the cage to it.

My dahlias are mostly in purple, red and pink shades, though they come in a much wider color range. 'Mystery Day' is an exotic beauty, an eight inch harlequin in purple and white. Combine it in a large vase with the dark purple 'Thomas Edison' and 'White Perfection' for a sumptuous display.

'Arabian Night' is a smaller plant with smaller flowers, almost black in the center blending into dark red toward the edge. 'Red Pygmy', perhaps my favorite, is smaller still. It grows comfortably in a twelve inch pot on a sunny deck, where it will flower copiously from July until frost in a color that makes you really understand what "red" means.

You can buy from a specialist, but I have collected mine over the years by visiting the racks in the megamarts each spring. They often come packaged two or three to a bag, so take a friend with you, buy several different varieties, and split them.

Though stores sell them in spring, truth is that this is the time to shop for the best bargains in dahlias, and here's how you do it. Visit a friend's garden and say (you should practice this at home), "My, what a beautiful dahlia. Where did you buy that? I'd like to buy one for my garden." Your friend will almost certainly offer to give you a tuber as soon as the season ends.

This works for three reasons. First, because no one ever takes my advice to put the plant's source on the garden label, so your friend probably has no idea where it came from.

Second, dahlias multiply. A single root planted in spring results in a clump several times the size in fall. It doesn't take long to run out of space to grow them.

Third, dahlia tubers aren't hardy. They have to be dug up in fall, after hard frost kills the tops, and stored over the winter. Since there won't be enough space to plant all of them next spring, most gardeners think, Better you store them than me. So you shouldn't be hesitant to hint broadly.

Besides price, there are other reasons to shop this way. You get to see the plant in full bloom instead of trusting the picture on the package. You can see the size of the plant, which may or may not be four feet. And you can see one thing the package in the store rarely tells you: the stem length. Since dahlias are so perfect to cut and bring indoors, you want long stems. Otherwise you have these huge dinnerplate flowers schlumping with their chins on the rim of the vase like sullen teens at the dinner table.

Dahlias are not winter hardy here, so they must be stored. The potted ones are easy to store. Just stick the pots, soil and all, in a cool basement and keep them dry.

Those planted in the ground take a little more effort, but not a whole lot more. After frost I dig them up, let them dry in the sun for a couple of days, throw the clumps in a box, and put the box on the floor next to the pots. I don't even knock the soil off the clumps.

I have learned—the hard way, which is usually the best way—that dahlias tubers can be quite fussy about their storage conditions. They like it very cool with air that is not bone dry. This situation is not difficult to find in an elderly house with an unheated, damp basement.

Those unfortunate enough to live in a modern house have a problem. You don't have a musty old cellar, you have a warm, dry furnace room. Sad, but a burden you must live with.

If you are storing dahlia tubers in a warm, dry spot, you need to take extra precautions so that they do not shrivel up and die over the winter. Wash all the soil off the tubers and let them dry thoroughly. Package them in a plastic grocery bag with some wood shavings, the kind sold as kennel bedding in most megamarts. Even with this, you should check them every few weeks to make sure they don't dry out. If this still doesn't work for you, try dipping them in an antidesiccant like Wilt-Pruf.

Your storage temperature will determine when the tubers begin to sprout next spring, the warmer the earlier. But under any conditions it may sometimes be too early to plant out, which you should resist until May. I pot my early risers up in gallon containers and give them all the light I can until the weather mellows. If this is too much trouble, you can just let them sprout, but potting will give you earlier flowers.

When they first sprout, just little buds at the stem end of the tubers, it is time to divide the clumps. If they grew well last year, the larger mass of tubers can be carefully untangled and cut into two or three pieces (I use a serrated kitchen knife, but don't tell my wife), each with three or four sprouting "fingers." That will give you more to plant. Or to give to friends in hope of an offer of some treasure from their gardens.

Unpotted Plants

Jane, a onetime friend, once told me that she inevitably killed any house plant she tried. I got a plant from my light garden, gave it to her, and told her it was foolproof.

As we chatted for a few more minutes, the small plant she was holding slowly and inexorably collapsed. A look combined of horror and grief crept over her face.

It was a cruel trick, and I have since given up such antics. Well, mostly. The plant had been an exceptionally delicate begonia, raised and protected in a specially controlled, enclosed atmosphere. The devil made me do it.

There are, however, stunning plants that the most inept duffer can handle. And I'm not talking about dull philodendrons and the aptly named cast iron plant here. I'm talking flowers!

Paperwhite narcissus are an example. These are similar to our spring daffodils, except that they neither require nor do they

172

tolerate our winter weather. They come in either white or yellow shades. I recommend the white for the truly inept.

Kits with the bulbs, a cute little pot, and the growing medium will soon be flooding into stores, but good garden centers will also sell the bulbs bulk, and that is what you should buy. If you get there early, you can pick out the biggest, which will give you the most flowers.

Besides the bulbs, you will need two things: a bowl and some gravel. The bowl should be clear glass, wide enough to hold your bulbs shoulder to shoulder and about three times as tall as the bulbs. The gravel can be any aggregate of pebbles, from individually selected Japanese river stones to left over construction pea stone. The granite chips sold in bags for paths and such is ideal.

Half fill the glass bowl with stone, set the bulbs on the surface, and fill in around the bulbs with more stone. The tip of the bulb should just show and they should be an inch or two below the rim of the bowl. Root growth will push them up.

Now—and here is why you want the clear glass bowl instead of the cute little pottery thing that comes in the kits—pour in water until it just reaches the BOTTOM of the bulbs. Every few days you'll have to add a little water to maintain that level. In good light and normal room temperatures, you will have flowers in about six weeks. For sure.

There is one strange thing about paperwhites: the aroma. Some people call it heavenly, others can't abide being in the same room. It is perplexing, because there is no way to know if people perceive the scent as different, or if they smell the same thing, but some like it and some don't. (I, for example, have always found the scent of a distant skunk attack on a summer evening pleasant.)

Are paperwhites still more than you can handle? Then try colchicum. Here are the instructions for colchicum. Buy a bulb at

173

a major garden center or mail order bulb specialist. Set the bulb on your coffee table or kitchen counter. That's it.

Colchicum will bloom in pale lavender or white just sitting there. No pot, no water, nothing. Is that easy enough for you.

After it blooms, and before the ground freezes, you can plant it outside. Just dig a hole in reasonably decent soil and plant so the top is three inches below the surface. If that is too complicated, you can just throw it out. I think I'll send one to Jane.

LINNAEUS

OCTOBER

Horror

It was a fearsome sound. Not quite a scream. Quieter, more chilling. Somewhere between a creak and a moan, something between death and life. Our small dog whimpered at my feet.

I sat in the comfortable chair in my study, but I was not comfortable. The chill of impending fall drifted through the open window like an evil wraith as I awaited with apprehension the next ominous emanation to come from the darkness.

The garden outside that window had once been a friendly place, a bright place, a safe place, but not tonight. Tonight something horrible was happening, and I knew, yet I dared not let myself know.

I shivered. Was it just the night fog that stirred in the blackness beyond the window, at times opaque, at times parting just enough to give a terrifying hint of what might lie in wait there, lurking in the gloom? Or was the chill something more primordial, deep in the limbic brain, some genetic memory lingering from generation to generation and cursing gardeners since that first feral man put seed in soil.

We have bears here, but their sound, if threatening, is not so harrowing: the heavy stomp of footsteps, the hair-raising crash of overturned garbage. But bears don't make this small sound that crept under my skin leaving nothing but dread and goosebumps. And bears are gone by morning.

The open window was something I could no longer endure. I closed it, not with a bang, but carefully, softly so as not to attract attention from the dreadful presence that was out there, waiting for me, just as children lie still for fear of waking the monster under the bed.

I know I will not sleep this night. I know that I dare not even close my eyes else the ghastly visions will play on the insides of my

eyelids like some gruesome horror movie, only worse: a horror movie I have lived, a horror movie I could not bear to live again. Besides, I needed to be awake, to think, to plan, somehow to find a way of dealing with the hellish fiend awaiting me.

My fear mixed with guilt, like sweat with blood on the rack, because I knew that I had caused it, created it. Just as the good Doctor Frankenstein had crafted his perfect man, only to have it turn against him, I could not escape my culpability for this beast. Like the thump thump thump from under the floorboards, this odious sound was all the more terrifying because it cried out my guilt.

It is no comfort to know that I do not tremble alone tonight. In this small town of unlocked doors, doors are locked and curtains drawn as summer dies, and doorbells go unanswered. Even those who have not summoned the demon themselves live in dread of the demons their once kindly, once conscionable neighbors have conjured up.

There it is again, that fingernail on the blackboard screech. The dog whines again, and I shudder.

Because, you see, I know well that rending sound. I know what it means. I have heard it before, and always with bone chilling terror. It is the small, anguished scream of tortured skin stretching as the creature inside expands, the ghastly groan that mocks my spring enthusiasm and my summer indolence.

I yearn for frost. It is the stake through the heart of this malignant plant. But even then the sinister seed bides in the corpse, eager to arise like the living dead next spring.

Good intentions lead us down dark alleys, and abomination masked as ardor abides in the hearts of gardeners. As I shiver and sweat, I swear once again that I will ruthlessly rogue out the malevolent spawn as the warming soil of spring urges it back to loathsome life. And that I will not—I ... WILL! ... NOT!—plant more than one zucchini.

Begonias

Begonias are the Rodney Dangerfield of houseplants. They don't get no respect. Tell someone you collect begonias and they look at you as if you told them you collect used chewing gum. But there are literally thousands of species and varieties of begonias, and one of them, *Begonia heracleifolia*, is guilty of shoving me down the road that led eventually to a house full of plants.

Three decades ago, while visiting a friend, I mumbled a few gratuitous words about her houseplant. A tall, gangly, and ugly thing—the plant, not Phyllis, who is a lady deserving of Heaven except for her one sin of sending me home with a begonia slip.

Before I knew it I had three hundred different varieties of begonias growing in our small house. Not only plants, but begonia paintings and begonia chachkas and every book ever written about begonias save one. (If you have the Eva Kenworthy Gray 1930 edition, call me.) It reached the point that my wife told me that the begonias must go or else she would. When she heard my reply, and particularly the alacrity of my reply, she reconsidered.

We reached an accommodation; it was that or starve to death. I got rid of most of the begonias by attrition, simply not replacing the ones that died. It took about a month. That made room for other plants, which were not covered by our covenant, and so it began. But a few begonias refused to die and are still here.

For me to have a houseplant that has survived my care for that long stretches credulity. To have half a dozen such survivors in the same plant family is unimaginable. And finally, that these survivors are elegant and exotic, true connoisseurs' plants, gives me a credibility quotient down near some news media outlets. But that's begonias for you. Delicate as they look, they are tough customers.

The most familiar is the wax begonia, *Begonia semperflorens*, sold by the millions in six packs every spring. They are touted as shade loving annuals, but they are actually sun tolerant perennials. Perhaps a bit of midday shade is in order, but generally the more

sun, the more flowers. My particular favorite is a bedding variety called 'Vodka'; with strong light the leaves turn almost black, making the bountiful red flowers really jump out.

This plant is just about foolproof, but also an easy and rewarding houseplant. In fact it is one of the few plants that will actually tolerate the Stewartesque recommendation of digging up a bedding plant and bringing it inside in fall. It will bloom for you all winter, and in spring you can take cuttings and start all over again.

Another stunning summer plant is the tuberous begonia, a standout in the shade garden. New gardeners are often so enthralled with their huge blossoms in bright colors that they bring the pots inside in fall. Bad idea. Tuberous begonias need a dormancy period in winter. If you have one still growing, stop watering it and let the top die back. Don't water again until you see sprouts in spring (page 51).

Wax and tuberous begonias are primarily outdoor plants, though. The real sirens of this diverse family are the less common houseplant varieties. There are a dozen different groupings, but the most alluring are the angle wing, sometimes called cane type, and the rhizomatous. (Don't just mumble past that; it's pronounced rye-ZOM-a-tus.) They grow, would you believe, from rhizomes, thickened stems that creep along the soil surface and spill gracefully over the side of the pot.

Your grandmother had an angel wing begonia; I'm sure of it. They're tall plants with leaves shaped like wings, often silvery spotted. They were popular in Victorian times because they bloomed reliably in the middle of winter with pendulous umbels (that means clusters of flowers that hang down) in shades of red, pink, white, or orange.

Since Grandma's day the breeders have been hard at work improving the strain. Leaves that put Christmas ornaments to shame and huge flower heads would make Grandma green with envy. And though they were undemanding a century ago, they are now even easier. This is clearly a plant to build a duffer's confidence.

The rhizomatous begonias are just as easy and even more dramatic. I have a friend who claims to be a gardener but turns her nose up in disdain at houseplants. During several visits this summer I noticed her staring like a hungry cat at one called 'Muddy Waters'—olive and pale green leaves with a red edge so deeply ruffled that they look like a wadded ball of lace. When I eventually offered her a rooted cutting, she jumped at it.

That is the best way to get these uncommon begonias—bug a friend until he gives you a piece. Fortunately they are easy to root. A small piece of the rhizome with two or three leaves attached can be pushed into a small pot with soilless potting mix augmented with some extra Perlite or vermiculite for good drainage. Put a bread bag over it to maintain humidity and keep it in good light but no direct sun. It will soon root. If you are not fortunate enough to have such discriminating friends, Logee's Greenhouses in Danielson, Connecticut, a candy shop for begoniacs, has hundreds of enticing varieties (www.logees.com).

Hundreds? Yes, there are hundreds of named varieties and dozens of species in the rhizomatous class alone. It would be futile to try to list even a sampling. (But you wouldn't go wrong with 'Madame Queen'.) All I can say is that if you see any at all in a nursery, plunk down three or four bucks and take one home. A small plant in a three inch pot will grow into a basketball sized stunner in a year, even with inept care. Trust me; I know.

The only place you might go wrong in growing any begonia is the soil. They need a humusy, well drained soil. I start with bagged soil and mix in a generous helping of ground bark and compost for plants that have reached the size for a ten-inch pot where they can stay for a while. Smaller plants get by with a peat-based mix right out of the bag.

In summer they go outside on the porch or under a tree. They need ample water and a regular fertilizer routine then, but in winter they prefer to stay on the dry side, and they'll take all the sun they can get during the dreary months. Normal house temperatures are fine, but they'll really thrive in a cool room.

An exception to this are the rex begonias, the "king" of the genus, rainbow leafed wonders that look more like Tiffany jewels than plants. They like warm temperatures, into the 70s during the day and no cooler than 60 at night, and they hate direct sun, even in winter. I do not have any twenty year old rexes in this cool house. But they're so sensational that I keep sneaking new ones in under my coat.

Most begonias are a natural for the fluorescent light garden, but especially the rexes. The metallic colors in the leaves glow with their own light.

If you succumb to the derangement of begonia collecting, there is a support group. The American Begonia Society brings together similarly afflicted people from around the country to talk about their problem, exchange information and cuttings, and learn more about their disorder.

There is debate whether begonias are actually addictive. I was able to quit cold turkey, and the tremors went away within a few weeks. I can now even grow the occasional social begonia. But I must admit that in moments of weakness I still dream of a time when the whole house was a wall-to-wall foliar fantasy.

Deadly Doses

Hi. My name's Duane, and I'm a biblioholic. But I'm getting help. When I have the urge to read a book, I can call my sponsor; he comes over, and we get drunk together.

I have books hidden all over the house, including hundreds of gardening books. But I have never had a book like the one an enabling friend dropped off the other night. It's called *Deadly Doses—a Writers Guide to Poisons* by Serita Deborah Stevens with Anne Klarner. I must shamefully admit that I fell off the library cart.

What does poisoning have to do with gardening? A lot. Just read Agatha Christie. (I used to, but I'm recovering.) She and her cohorts are always bumping people off with oleander.

 According to *Deadly Doses*, that is not fiction. Oleander, a house plant in the Northeast and a common street tree in warmer climates, is deadly dangerous. Ingestion can be almost instantly fatal, and even honey made by bees that frequent oleander can be toxic.

But you don't have oleander, do you, so what's the problem?

Maybe you have a nice shady patch of lily of the valley. Beautiful in the spring. And deadly. Or rhododendrons and azaleas. Ditto. And you know those pulpy red berries on the yew hedges that are scattered around just about every neighborhood in the country? Contrary to what we were told as kids, they're not very toxic. But every other part of the plant is lethal.

Frequently in this space I have sung the praises of castor beans, always with the caveat that it is deadly if you eat the seeds. I know many people will not grow this beautiful and dramatic annual because of that, but can you poison proof your yard, your neighborhood, the nearby woods?

No. Truth is that we live in a dangerous world, and we always have. Humans have coexisted with these deadly doses for hundreds of thousands of years, learning the hard way what to eat and what to keep well clear of.

But *Deadly Doses* is not a book about plants, it's a book about poisons, and only a quarter of the book involves our gardens and wildernesses. In 1800 about 90 percent of poisonings, accidental or intentional, were caused by plants. Today, with perverse thanks to progress, this is down to seven percent.

There is a chapter on pesticides, a short one, and one that deals largely with the more dangerous restricted chemicals used by farmers and professional applicators. Only a few compounds available to the home owner make the list. And though they are

nothing you would want to mix into your morning coffee (nor would it do you much good to mix it in someone else's), these are often less dangerous than the plants we spray them on.

If we are not dying or being done in in large numbers today by plants or pesticides, what is the mystery writer to turn to? The most fecund field would be medicines. Medicines are often poisons used in sub-lethal doses, and we willingly swallow them —while protesting the three parts per billion pesticide residue on our broccoli.

Another fertile field to explore would be right under the sink or on the shelves in the garage and basement. Many household products we use casually every day are very dangerous things. I often wonder how dedicated organic gardeners differentiate between the poisons they will not tolerate on their flowers and the equally dangerous poisons they use to clean their houses.

Anyway, it is an interesting book for all of you who want to write mysteries. Or create mysteries. Now, where can I hide this so my wife won't find it.

DDT

I have listened to *Man of La Mancha* on my Walkman several times in the last few days. It's good leaf raking music. I arrange to be in the garage or the garden shed during the last scene, though, because it always leaves me misty-eyed. I'm a sucker for lost causes fought bravely, for tilting against windmills and failing with dignity.

This has inspired me to lower my lance against the popular perception of DDT. You remember DDT? The insecticide that was banned in 1972 because...because...well, that's the question. You think you know the answer, something to do with bird eggs and building up in the environment and cancer, but you'd be wrong.

DDT was patented as the first safe and effective insecticide in 1939. Nine years later Paul Muller received the Nobel Prize in

Medicine for that discovery. Medicine? Yes, because in that short time DDT had already saved millions of lives. It was a miracle!

Some of the world's most virulent diseases—malaria, typhus, bubonic plague—are transmitted by insects. Kill the insects and you stop the disease.

 More soldiers in World War I died from typhus, carried by lice, than from enemy action. In World War II lavish use of DDT allowed tens of thousands of our GIs to return home, perhaps your father or grandfather. You may owe your very existence to DDT.

Malaria killed two million people every year before DDT. In Sri Lanka alone reported cases went from 2,800,000 per annum before DDT down to 15 after DDT. And when DDT use came to a panic stop, cases rocketed right up again to 2.5 million.

But it harms birds, right? Wrong. Egg shell thinning was shown in some studies, not in others, but you didn't read about the others. Repeatability is the essence of proof in science, but the egg allegations are still being bandied about as gospel by people who have never looked at any of the studies, and certainly not those that indicated otherwise.

The truth is that egg shell thinning had been observed for decades before DDT. It is caused by many environmental factors, but probably not by DDT. In laboratory tests birds fed massive quantities of DDT over their reproductive life showed no significant decline in hatching rates. In some cases the "poisoned" birds had higher hatch rates than the control group.

I was once moderator of a large Internet discussion group overweighted with aging hippies and former biology majors. Biology grad students are the slave labor for university research labs. When I mentioned the egg shell fallacy I received two private emails from two different people, both requesting anonymity, who had worked on studies back then which showed no effect from DDT, and in both cases their professors had been unable to publish. It didn't fit the narrative.

Then why did bird populations fall so precipitously during the years of heavy DDT use? That's easy. They didn't.

Birders may know that the Audubon Society conducts a bird count every Christmas. With the exception of a handful of raptors, whose decline was almost certainly due to loss of habitat and has since been reversed, bird populations went up between the late 1930s and the late 1960s, often markedly.

Cancer? Forget it. Two groups of humans were fed 15,000 times the normal dose daily for 27 months. No effect. Follow-up thirty years later—still no effect. Pesticide applicators, the most vulnerable group—no effect.

Environmental build-up? An argument fed by our increasing ability to detect infinitesimal amounts. Even to the extent that build up might be observable, no observable effects are found. Residue in fatty tissue of humans? Yes, but so what. Vitamin A, a known carcinogen, does the same thing. Absolutely no harmful effects have been seen from common trace amounts of DDT in the human body.

After Rachel Carson published *Silent Spring,* a book of near poetry but highly questionable science, the infant Environmental Defense Fund pressured the Department of Agriculture to ban DDT. Ag did a major study and held hearings and declined. The EDF then went to the new Environmental Protection Agency with the same request and the same results. Big study, no ban. Finally William Ruckelshaus bowed to pressure, ignored his own studies and commissions, and issued the ban. Why? Ten years later he admitted it was pure politics.

Egg shell thinning and environmental buildup can be argued as long as you understand that they are contested. Poorly supported suggestions of human harm, including cancer, are less probative. Here are facts that even DDT opponents do not deny:

1. No human death or disease has ever been recorded from exposure to DDT, and by "no" I mean not one, zero, nada. This, in spite of the fact that in the early days of DDT use hundreds of millions were indiscriminately exposed to massive doses, often on

a monthly basis, and scientific study participants were fed—FED!—DDT at thousands of times the potential environmental exposure with no ill results.

2. Millions of lives were saved by DDT use, and since the world stopped using it, tens of millions of people have died unnecessarily. Tens of millions dead. It dwarfs the Nazi holocaust.

These statistics are not denied by DDT opponents, just ignored. Don't you think it should be part of the debate? Don't you think that windmill should be at least wounded?

October Chores

A friend of mine has a theory. He explains that when you are ten years old, a year is ten percent of your life. When you are fifty years old, a year is only two percent of your life. Two percent of your life goes by much more quickly than ten percent, and that's why time, the seasons, the years race by when you get older. Late enough in the evening, it made sense.

The bad side of this is that summer passes in a flash. The good side is that winter goes by nearly—but not quite—as quickly. October is almost Christmas, and Christmas is almost spring. So October is almost the start of gardening season.

Granted, this year's garden is still sorta there where you can see it, and that's good. You can evaluate what went wrong. By next April you will have forgotten what you screwed up. At least, I would.

Some shrubs in the mixed border have leaves marred by a fungus. I don't know exactly which fungus, but it doesn't matter. Part of the problem was this summer's weather, a petri dish for fungus, but some of it was that they need pruning out for better air circulation. That's a good job for fall.

Surprisingly the large patch of Volcano phlox had almost no mildew, even though the weather begged for it, even though I didn't get around to thinning the stems in spring as I should. Volcano is resistant to mildew, but this summer was the acid test, and it passed.

Still, the operative words here are "large patch." We're talking about a serious need for dividing and thinning out. Another good job for Indian summer, or I guess it's Native American summer now, after the first hard frost.

These little jobs, so obvious to me now, will be forgotten in a few weeks when the time comes to do them. I tied a ribbon of florescent plastic tape, unsticky flagging tape from a building supply, on the future jobs. When leaves fall, these bright, fluttering mnemonics will leap out from the brown landscape to remind me.

Some plants are just in the wrong place despite my brilliant plans. A 'Kopper King' hibiscus, with dinner plate pink blooms on dusky foliage, was intentionally grown behind much taller Scotch thistle. It seemed like a good idea at the time.

The Scotch thistle grows to seven or eight feet by early summer, a stately giant with large, silvery leaves. It blooms with typical purple thistle flowers in July, spills seeds all over the place, and then ages like a morph shot in a horror movie. So in July I would cut it down, unveiling the hibiscus, just in time for its August extravaganza. That was the plan.

When I cut the thistles down, I found the hibiscus had grown weak and flowerless in their shade. The thistle had to be in back. No problem. You don't plant Scotch thistle, you unplant it. It reseeds all over your garden, and you pull out the ones you don't want. A job for next spring. I'll tie a ribbon on the hibiscus to remind me to move it forward.

This is probably the only real slow time in a garden, so I'm going to do what I always swear I'm going to do—redo labels. After decades of faded ink and brittle plastic, I have finally found a system that works. Narrow slat Venetian blinds are cheap, and the vinyl is formulated to stand up to the sunlight that destroys plastic labels in a couple of seasons. They cut easily with scissors, and you can make them long or short for botanical or common names.

Iberis saxatilis

And forget Magic Markers; you know they fade. Paint pens from an art store are the only things that stand up. I'll have to hurry. Slow time passes quickly. Spring is almost here.

Trial by Death

There are two ways to be successful with house plants. Method I: You put a lot of effort into producing just the right conditions for them. Or Method II: You get plants that will endure the conditions you already have.

Method II has two variations. Method II-a: You study your conditions and read up on plants and make careful choices. Or Method II-b: You buy whatever plants catch your fancy and let them tell you which are right for your house. Those will be the ones that live.

Many people have used II-b without knowing it. In the absence of official sanction, they call it killing plants and universally whine that they have a brown thumb. Now that death is part of a named and published technique (I even capitalized "Methods" to lend more authority), the duffers' self esteem should improve, something I'm told is key in support groups.

A couple of winters ago I was sitting on the sun porch with a friend. He glanced around and said, "You must be quite a gardener!" Well, I was stunned. No one had ever spoken those words in my direction before.

After I recovered, I asked him why he thought that. He said, "Because you have so many really big plants; you must have kept them alive for a long time." As a Method II-b gardener, I didn't argue with him; I didn't invite him to examine my compost pile, either.

I am reminded of Dean Martin's famous line. A man was bragging about his drinking prowess. Martin said condescendingly, "Son, I spill more than you drink."

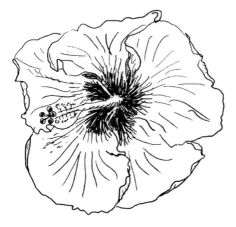

Like Dean Martin...sort of...I kill more plants than most people grow. And I feel good about that. By golly, I really do feel good about it. But not so good that I want to kill more than I have to.

It only makes sense that you put as much effort as you can spare into Method II-a before moving on to II-b. That means you do a minimal amount of research. You can cut your losses, for instance, by knowing not to put a fern on a radiator or a citrus in a dark corner behind the wing chair.

I have griped in the past about the lack of a good encyclopedic book on house plants. I now submit, with something short of overwhelming enthusiasm, The *RHS Encyclopedia of House Plants* as perhaps the best of a mediocre lot. At thirty-five bucks it's expensive, perhaps, but not too bad for a four-pound book packed with information and colour (it's British, you know) photos. The enthusiast would want a copy, but others will look for it in their local library.

For each plant it gives the basics in a series of symbols right up front. You see what temperatures a plant needs (cool, moderate, or warm), the exposure (full sun, half sun, shade), water requirements and whether it is suitable for home growing or needs a conservatory. So you can get a quick idea without even reading any words.

With this rough information you can choose plants that at least have a fighting chance and place them in an appropriate part of your home. That will cut your losses. Keep in mind that you can also move a house plant that is not doing well. A plant languishing in one spot may thrive a few feet away. Plants seldom explain why.

Pure Method II-b gardening is not for the faint of heart. You must be able to live with failure. You must decide. (Get ready—you've been expecting this.) II-b or not II-b; that is the question.

For many, it is not a question at all. It is an imperative. Such gardeners can comfort themselves on their next trip to the compost pile with the thought that they are at least practicing a legitimate horticultural method. And that they have lots of company.

Half Time

Fall is a difficult time for me, as it is for many men. A conflicted time. There is work to be done in the garden, and the weather is fine for it, but Saturday is college football and Sunday the pro games.

It's not as bad as soccer. With soccer you need to bring a cooler into the TV room with 45 minutes plus a little more worth of supplies, because if you go to the refrigerator you might miss the only three seconds of action in the entire half. Football at least has time outs.

Injuries and reviewed calls are the best. You can count on three or four minutes to run outside and do something. Not much, but something.

In two minutes you can rush out and cut some ripened seed heads onto a small tray, then bring them to clean in front of the television. Or you can pull maybe five weeds. It's even enough time to plant some lettuce seeds. Or pick some tomatoes.

Then there's the lawn. A time out gives you enough time to call a lawn care company.

You can sprinkle some fertilizer and spade up a square foot of ground, ready to plant a dozen tulips at the next time out.

After three or four frantic forays out to the garden, half time seems to be an eternity. Imagine what you can do with this luxurious excess of time.

I don't think Tom Christopher and Marty Asher had football in mind when they wrote *The 20-Minute Gardener*—otherwise they would have called it *The 15-Minute Gardener*—but they have lots

189

of quick projects that will fit if you rush. And it is an easy and funny read, written in short sections that you can read in situations where you only want a page or two at a time, like in that small reading room at the top of the stairs. Or during shorter time outs.

Some of their projects are farfetched and take 20 minutes the way a football game takes one hour. They fudge by not counting a couple of hours of preparation. But still the book is fun and full of some really good ideas. Like building a window box, as long as you have all the pieces cut beforehand.

My half time excursions are more pedestrian. I like to use that time for open ended tasks, things you can do without doing all of. Pruning shrubs and deadheading roses and dahlias, for instance.

Since it is fall, the house plants need some attention before they come inside for the winter, about ten minutes attention. I clean all the summer debris off the soil surface and remove dead leaves. Sometimes I cut back their more exuberant summer growth. And I scrub down the clay pots with a wire brush.

Plants outside get stuff in them and on them. I like to bring nature inside, but not all of nature. So I wash them thoroughly with a hose. With large tough plants I use the jet setting. More delicate plants get the mist setting used close up. I make sure to get under the leaves and into the leaf axils.

The next step is optional, depending on your gardening theology. I spray them with a systemic insecticide. Sometimes that gets them through almost to Christmas before the bugs come back.

I don't fertilize plants I'm bringing in early. It's like eating a huge meal right before going to bed. But those that will stay out for a few weeks longer, particularly summer bulbs that will be dug and stored, get their last feeding, an easy half-time job.

Whatever little job I do, I'm back inside for the second half kick-off. I get a little bit done, but more important, this minimal activity takes the edge off my wife's pique at seeing me glued to the couch, never venturing further than the fridge, all weekend.

NOVEMBER

Garden Ornaments

This time of year I go looking for garden ornaments. I look in stores for half price summer clearance, way back in the corner behind the plastic Christmas trees now, or for items in the new Christmas line, and I look in my own garden for ornaments that got lost under the summer's growth.

I have strong feelings about garden ornaments. As a general rule, they should have no moving parts. They should make no sound heard beyond your property line. People have been acquitted of wind chime homicides by sympathetic juries of people who had been similarly abused.

And they most certainly should not have audio computer chips activated by motion sensors. In fact, those shouldn't even be on store shelves. Any store manager who allows croaking frogs on a main aisle should be required to put one just inside his office door, too.

There are four acceptable materials, concrete, wood, metal, and the recent composites that look very much like stone. Sometimes ceramic. You will notice one common material conspicuously missing from this list.

Though my approach is prescriptive, I do not disdain whimsy. Gnomes and duck families have their place in some settings. My tolerance of whimsy is not generous enough, however, to allow sheets of plywood cut and painted to look like...well, you know.

Gazing balls have become popular again, and though some put them in the same class as pink flamingos, I don't. My grandmother had a gazing ball, and she had the good sense to use it as it was intended to be used.

191

Gazing balls do not want to sit in the middle of the lawn with wax begonias around the base. They are not out there so you can check your makeup. They want to be in an overplanted border, ideally a cottage style garden, reflecting a tangle of tall flowers.

If once a month or so you need to cut back the flowers in order to see the globe, you have it in the right place. If most of what you see reflected is sky and the neighbor's yard, it is the wrong place.

In the same scale are birdbaths and sundials. The same rule applies to birdbaths. A birdbath standing in the middle of the lawn not only looks out of place, but the birds don't like it either. Would you take a bath in the middle of your yard? Never mind, I don't want to know. But birds want their baths near the shelter of small trees or shrubs.

Sundials are only slightly different. For obvious reasons they need to be in a spot where the sun hits them. Maybe that has to be in the middle of the lawn, but before giving in to the cliché, look around for a spot that gives them some context.

Arbors and gates may be on sale now, especially floor models. If you luck out on a good price on a floor model, here's one piece of advice. Make sure you get the instruction book that originally came with it. Trust me. It's important. I know. Now.

I have the same gripe about arches and gates that I have about gazing balls and birdbaths: They are too often stuck in the wrong place. Let's say you ran into a really good deal on a front entrance door, real oak with stained glass and solid brass hardware at a price you couldn't pass up. But would you take it home and set it up in the middle of your living room?

Dumb as it sounds, people do exactly that with arbors. Arbors, especially those with gates, must lead someplace. They need to think they have a purpose. It's a self esteem issue. If you don't have a place for them to lead to, consider your bargain an opportunity to

192

make one. Plop it in the middle of the lawn and start building a whole new garden beyond it.

These are all fairly large items, but most of my garden ornaments are small and at least partly hidden. I tuck pieces in here and there so that you discover them, not have them leap out at you.

Now I must find them. They may be advertised as frostproof, but I don't believe it. I bring them inside for the winter.

Many aren't even dew proof. A summer or two outside and the color starts to wash away. A little of that is good. I like the distressed look. But when they have reached a point of dissolution I find attractive, I spray them with clear exterior polyurethane to stop it. If you like the original colors, you can do that at the start.

Though even expensive ornaments can have the paint wash off, it is particularly true of schlock. I use this word endearingly, for one man's schlock is another's art. And I am not ashamed to say that many of the small gewgaws in my garden cost only a dollar, from stores of the same name.

Toad houses, for instance. I have two or three tucked into inconspicuous spots in the border, though I am not sure that they work any better than the halves of broken terra cotta pots that I put

in the garden. What else can you do with broken pots? Truth be known, I have never caught a toad hiding in any of them. I finally gave up and bought a dollar store toad to put in my dollar store toad house. No one can see it, but I know it's there.

I'm partial to these little things tucked in here and there. But the key phrase here is "tucked in." You can have a whole menagerie of cheap animals in the garden as long as they aren't visible all at once. A green frog sitting on the back step can be tacky. Peeking out from under a plant it isn't, at least not as much.

Stepping stones are another cutesy item, once expensive, now cheap enough to buy several and sold everywhere. Some are

sublimely ugly, others more tolerable. I like them in the lawn, sometimes alone, sometimes leading somewhere in a random wandering fashion. I toss them where I think I want them and then look at the placement for a couple of days—maybe weeks—until I'm sure. Then I run a knife around the edge, cutting and removing an appropriate sized piece of turf. That way they are at grass level and I can mow over them.

Pots can be ornaments, or they can just be something to put plants in. It's a fine line. Several pots bunched together need to be innocuous, almost disappearing under the effect of the plants. But one pot or tub standing by itself can be more flashy. And a concrete or plaster pillar makes it even more special.

I like to put decorative pots with exactly the right plant out in the garden, but they don't sit on the ground where slugs can crawl in and mud can splash up. On the other hand, I can't afford a pillar for each one. So I build up a low platform of bricks, salvaged and free of course, one foot square and two or three bricks high. On top I put a 12-inch tile from a building supply, commonly on sale for less than a dollar. It makes the potted plant a feature instead of something just sitting there.

All of these things come inside to protect them from what we have coming. They'll be good until Thanksgiving, but it might take me that long to find them.

Raised Vegetable Bed

A friend recently asked me how to start a raised bed vegetable garden. (What's that, dear?) I'm sorry; I stand corrected. A friend recently asked my wife to ask me how to start a raised bed vegetable garden.

This would be her first garden. (Yes, dear?) All right, she had tried a vegetable garden before and failed dismally. (What?) OK, not dismally, but it wasn't a great success. Excuse me a sec while I close my study door.

There. Anyway, this friend picked the right time to ask, because building a great vegetable garden is a job for fall, not spring. It's like laying out your clothes at night, so everything is ready bright and early. If you wait until spring, the ground is soggy, so is the weather, and by the time you've got your new garden ready you've missed half the season.

Her reason for asking early was that she had an extensive garden in mind, but I'm going to talk her into something smaller: a single four foot by eight foot bed. That space will provide more food than you can imagine, and the small scale will allow the job to be done right. Most important, it won't leave you so lame that you'll never garden again.

First, choose a site with full sun. (Full sun, yeah, yeah.) LISTEN TO ME! If there are large trees or a garage or barn on the eastern edge of your garden, you will miss several hours of morning sun. On the west you miss the late afternoon sun. On the south, you miss spring.

OK, not all of us are blessed with sun from dawn till dark. But for every hour of direct sunlight lost, you reduce production and you wait longer for your first ripe tomatoes. So think about the site, look around, watch the sun. Pick the best spot you have, not the first spot you think of.

Given the unlikely choice between two good locations, pick the one closest to the house, maybe a place you walk by on the way to the car. That way you can check every day and cut short fast-developing problems like weeds and diseases and insects. I know: Even if the garden is way out behind the garage, you will check it every day, of course you will. But you won't. Put it close.

You'll need three eight-foot 2 by 8's, either pressure treated for around 25 bucks or plain, which is cheaper but more expensive. That is, it costs less to buy, but you need to replace it every few

195

years. Anyway, your choice. You'll want at least four bags of ground pine bark mulch, probably a bag of lime, a bag of 5-10-5 fertilizer, maybe a package of superphosphate or bonemeal. Total, forty some dollars, less than a dollar fifty a square foot to make soil that will last forever and make your neighbors jealous.

Cut one of your eight-foot pieces of lumber into two four-foot pieces. If you don't have a saw or a neighbor with a saw, the lumber yard will do this for you. Now you have four pieces for the price of three, so you're saving money already. Screw them together with three long stainless steel screws or lag bolts in each corner. I like to paint, or better still, stain the finished frame. This should be a beautiful garden, not just a bountiful one.

Put your frame in the spot you've selected, step back and admire it. You've just built a raised bed. You probably think the hard part is over. You probably think you just pour some dirt in it and you're ready to go, right?

Of course not. That would be too easy. Like hand cranking homemade ice cream, anything tastes better if you put a preposterous amount of effort into it. We're going to double dig that sucker.

Double digging is an exercise invented by gardeners of past generations to punish their children. It creates a deep, rich soil bed, so the roots can grow down, not out. You can plant closer together, and the roots go deep where the water supply is more reliable.

You will be digging only 32 square feet; you can do that. And you'll be doing it on a nice day in November, cool and bright. If you survive, you can make a second bed next fall.

To start, take a handful of lime and sprinkle it lightly around the outside of your frame; then set the frame aside. The lime marks your work space.

Beginning in a corner, plunge a spading fork into the ground as deep as it will go and remove the clump of turf. Place the clump outside the limed outline. Continue doing this until you have a trench one fork deep and one fork wide along the end of the frame and a ridge of turf lying beside it. (You can remove the next layer and set this subsoil beside the row of turf, making a trench TWO forks deep, but I don't want to scare you.)

Into the bottom of the trench scatter a handful of superphosphate or bonemeal, a handful of 5-10-5 fertilizer, a dusting of lime and a large bucket or two of ground bark mulch. Spade it in. You should also dig in any organic matter you have; remember, you will never see this soil again. Perhaps you can find a few leaves lying around this time of year; hit 'em once or twice with the lawn mower to chop them up and dig them into the trench. Compost is great, or rotted manure, even sawdust. How much organic matter is enough? Dig in all you can manage. Then dig in some more. It's still not enough, but it will have to do.

On to step two. Right next to your first trench, dig a second. This time put the turf chunks you dig out into the bottom of the first trench, turf side down, and break them up a bit. Remove any stones too large to fall through the tines of the fork. Some perfectionists remove all the stones, but I'm giving instructions for the merely dedicated, not the demented.

Dig all the good stuff into the bottom of Trench Two as you did before and move on to Trench Three. Keep going.

When you get to the end of the bed, fill the last trench with the stuff you set aside from the first trench.

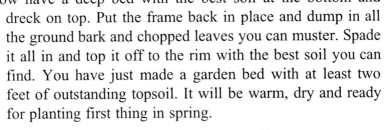

You now have a deep bed with the best soil at the bottom and dreck on top. Put the frame back in place and dump in all the ground bark and chopped leaves you can muster. Spade it all in and top it off to the rim with the best soil you can find. You have just made a garden bed with at least two feet of outstanding topsoil. It will be warm, dry and ready for planting first thing in spring.

Pat yourself on the back—if you can still move your arms.

How much can you grow in a 4 by 8 foot bed? A lot, a whole lot.

As soon as the snow melts, scatter some lettuce seeds across the four foot end. Move down a foot and scatter some spinach. Throw in a few radish seeds. When the weather mellows a bit in April, put in some broccoli transplants. Maybe a couple cabbages (small ones). But these are just appetizers.

When frost is past, put two tomato plants in cages at the end opposite where the lettuce is growing. Scatter some more lettuce or radish seeds around them; you'll eat that before the tomatoes get big enough to crowd them out. That fills the first eight square feet.

Three pepper plants, placed in a triangle take the next 2- by 2-foot section. Opposite them scatter some carrot seeds. You won't get a lot of carrots, but in my rocky clay, it's amazing to grow carrots at all. That's another eight square feet.

Divide the next couple of feet into 1- by 2-foot sections. Pick what you want: onions, beets, hot peppers, herbs, more cabbages, bush cucumber, eggplants. parsley, parsnips, chard. When the heat of summer wipes out the lettuce you planted in April, rip it out and plant some beans. And in September when you've eaten the beans and carrots, scatter some more lettuce and spinach seed.

You won't do a lot of canning, but you'll get good food for the summer. And next fall you might have recovered enough to put in another raised bed.

African Violets

Give me the choice between an African violet and a begonia, I'll take the begonia every time. Give me the choice between an African violet and ... oh, say a well grown poison ivy? Well, poison ivy has its charms, red stemmed and glossy. It would be a tough decision.

The problem is that I grew up in a house full of African violets at a time when African violets were nothing but sort of pinkish or sort of bluish things with fuzzy leaves. And there were dozens and dozens of them, all over, all pretty much the same.

Violets have changed over the years, maybe even improved (he admitted grudgingly). Still, there are none in my house. I have received some from time to time, but I always managed to kill them. My cataract surgeon traditionally gave patients an African violet for each eye. I had killed the first before I went back for the second surgery. I retaliated by giving him a sauromatum.

If you have African violets that you would like to kill, I can offer some tips.

Plant them in the wrong soil. Violets like a soil that is very open with a lot of organic matter. If you plant them in the store special potting mix, the heavy bags stacked up for a buck or so, you can joyfully watch them die a lingering death.

But say it's too late for that. Say you've already potted the thing up in a soil mixture specifically made for African violets, maybe added some extra home-brew compost. You can still find a way.

Potted in the soil they prefer, they are notoriously difficult to water. They like to be constantly slightly moist, not bone dry, not soaking. So if you water copiously every three or four days or let them go dry for a couple of weeks, you will shortly have nothing to worry about. Nothing at all.

As far as light is concerned, most people know instinctively what to do. Visiting friends, I often see violets sitting on an end table back in the dimmest corner of the room. After all, they're a "low light" plant, aren't they?

Actually they are a bright light plant. They'll take all the light you can give them short of direct summer sun. For those of you who attempt planticide by putting them in a sunny window in winter, it won't work. The sun isn't strong enough to be fatal. In fact, they'll love it and bloom their hearts out. But leave them in the same window as the spring sun gets stronger and you can bake 'em to death with ease.

A friend recently sent me a photo of a sick violet and asked me what was wrong. Nothing was wrong; it was nearly dead. But that wasn't what she was looking for. The pot was sitting on a

windowsill, and the flash reflected off the darkened window. The problem was obvious. She was trying to grow it at night.

African violets like humid air, like the window sill over the kitchen sink or a bathroom window. So for a quick death try putting them in a window right over a radiator or heat vent, where the air is desert-dry.

Real aficionados insist that you must water from the bottom, and I will agree with them. If you top water and get water on the leaves, it can leave ugly white spots, especially if the water is cold or if the plant sits in sun.

Why would I be so solicitous of the leaves? Unfortunately the water spotting does them no real harm; it just makes them look lousy. Since those following my regimen will have no flowers, you might as well have the leaves looking good as long as they last.

These leaves can get dusty, and a violet fancier lovingly dusts them using another violet leaf. Yeah, sure; like a real person is going to do that.

My first thought is to take the crevice tool of the vacuum to them, but that might be a little obvious. But here is the one exception to the no-water-on-the-leaves rule. You can hose them off in the kitchen sink as long as you use lukewarm water and let them dry completely before you put them back in the window.

Whatever you do, don't fertilize, and certainly not with a high phosphorus violet fertilizer. The new varieties can bloom almost year round if you feed them. If yours were to do that, you might actually get attached to it.

If you follow all of this advice and the plant still hangs on, here is the ultimate death sentence. Take a vacation for a couple of weeks and give the plant to a neighbor to watch.

Works every time.

Vacation Care

My mother is gone several years now, and I can finally tell this story. For many years Mother drove to Florida every fall and returned in spring. Such nomadic lifestyles have been bothersome for ten thousand years, ever since the domestication of plants. The prehistoric complication was wheat, but Mother's problem was a philodendron, a direct descendent of a plant her grandmother had tended and passed on. Ugly thing. The plant, that is, though my great grandmother was no beauty either. Still, Mother was attached to it and couldn't just leave it to die. So her son, the plant expert, got to baby-sit every winter, earning in return some new gewgaw made from shells to be prominently displayed when she visited, packed away in the attic when she left.

I hate philodendrons. Not with a passion—that would be too strong an emotion to squander on such a vapid plant—but I feel the ounce or two of water they need every week is a waste of natural resources. So though this plant had lived through three generations of inept care, and though I would start each October with good intentions, the family heirloom always died by Christmas.

No problem. Each spring I went out, bought a new philodendron and stuck it in Great Grandma's pot. Mother never noticed. People who have only one house plant are not terribly observant.

I think of that story every time I have to go away for a trip. It inspires me to find any possible way to get my plants through the experience without exposing them to the care of someone like me. If some simple measures are taken, most plants will survive a week or two without care. Some will take a month or two. And therein lies the first problem: You must know your plants' needs. A water glutton like hibiscus constrains your vacations more than a cactus.

Cactus and succulents will take several weeks untended on a winter windowsill without even breathing hard. They grew up with strong sun and little water. Leafy plants are less forgiving, but they'll go untended longer than you think. The first rule is to get them out of direct sun or strong light.

Plants dry out for a couple of reasons. One is evaporation from the soil surface. Even soil in an empty pot will dry out on its own.

A living plant causes it to dry even faster, because leafy plants transpire. That means they give off water through their leaves and replace it by drawing water out of the soil with their roots. They do this in response to light and temperature. So the lower the light level and temperature, the less transpiration and the longer your plant can go without watering.

It makes economic sense to lower the thermostat when you go away. But I know people who keep the heat up for the plants, thinking they don't like the chill. That's a mistake. Low 50s is fine for both the plants and the budget.

Light is a little trickier. You don't want Stygian gloom, but something dimmer than a windowsill. Look for a spot where daylight is bright enough to read by, but just barely. Your plants won't like it, but they'll survive. If you had to water once a week before, you can go two weeks or more in a cool, dim corner.

Another way to reduce transpiration is to increase the humidity in the air around the plant. A clear plastic garbage bag or one from the dry cleaner will do that. Just be certain that the sun NEVER hits it or you'll have stewed geraniums when you come home. They taste terrible.

For a large collection, the bathtub is a great vacation spot. They'll think you've sent them to a spa. Put empty pots upside down in the tub, put your houseplants on them, and fill the tub so it is just below the bottom of your houseplants. (This is a good time to fix the drain so it doesn't leak; you've been meaning to anyway, right?) Close the curtain or shower door and they'll love it. In fact, they might even look better by the time you get back.

Commercial self-watering containers work fairly well, though usually not as well as the advertising claims. They are particularly handy for plants too big to schlep into the tub. Just fill the reservoir, bag the top, and take off without worry.

Several self-watering tubs that I use on the patio in summer for annuals and tender bulbs sit unused in the garage during winter. For vacation care, I dig them out (if I can find them), fill them with potting soil, and bury small clay pots up to the rim in the soil. With the reservoir filled, the water will soak into the pots.

That method works best with clay, but capillary matting does the same job for both clay and plastic. Capillary matting systems are expensive, but I rigged up my own watering machine from yard sale booty. I lined a large commercial cookie tray with a piece of an old blanket, the cheap kind with lots of polyester. It was cut the width of the tray, but much longer so the end could hang down into the kitchen sink filled with water.

I prepare the pots by shoving a twisted hank of old panty hose into the hole in the bottom, leaving just enough hanging out to make contact with the wet blanket. The blanket sucks water up from the tub, and the hank-o'-hose transfers it to the soil. Not pretty, but it works. You can also use this method with pots stored in the bathtub for a lengthy hiatus.

Finally there are automatic watering systems, once very expensive but affordable now. A spaghetti-like tangle of capillary tubes and emitters and an automatic timer could theoretically relieve you of watering duties forever.

These techniques will get you through a medium length trip—a week or two or three. But for short absences, when it's not worthwhile to set everything up, or a lengthy expedition, you must ultimately resort to the herbicidal maniac next door. Or worse (ominous pause), A Relative! (Fade in violin shrieks from *Psycho*.)

When turning over care of your beloved leafy family to a drooling, shifty-eyed incompetent, you must do what you can to remove the element of judgment. Trusting in their horticultural skills is certain death.

Plants are normally grouped according to their light requirements. But for lengthy vacations I group them by water needs. Each cluster of plants is labeled with a file card giving days of

the week on which they are to be watered—"Saturday" for pots that need attention only once a week, "Tuesday & Saturday" for thirstier ones, and so on.

To prevent the bonehead from dumping the entire daily output of Niagara Falls on your plants every time she walks into the house, I impose discipline with my favorite watering tool, a battery filler. This four dollar gizmo from an auto supply store, which looks like an oversized turkey baster, does everything better than tools deliberately designed for watering.

With a battery filler you put exactly the amount of water you want exactly where you want it. No more dribbling on the floor or windowsill. It can provide a gentle stream for seed flats, and with pots where the top is obscured by healthy growth, the nose pokes through the foliage.

The file cards for each group of plants instruct your clueless caregiver how much water to give. One squeeze is just right for four inch pots, two squeezes for six inch, and so on. It would take deliberate malice to screw this up. Do not allow for any discretion. You can't expect much from people who work for T-shirts.

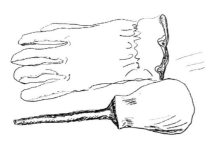

I don't go away often. People with a large plant collection and a variety of pets tend to hang close to home. But when I do, one or more of these procedures has held the death toll down to levels no worse than my plants experience under my own loving care. And sometimes better. I have on occasion returned to find a plant, on its last legs when I left, showing glowing good health. I think my neighbor has slipped in a few ringers to assuage a guilty conscience.

Top Ten List

The National Garden Bureau just put out a Top Ten list titled "Why Garden." I quickly looked down the list to see where "mental disease" fell.

It wasn't there. But there was enough there to cobble together a column the easy way.

Their Number One reason is "Garden for safe, healthy food." That is utter nonsense, of course. It plays to the organic cultists who believe that one picogram of pesticide residue on store-bought tomatoes can wipe out your family.

Drop the word "healthy" though and I agree completely with the conclusion. Garden for good food.

Some things are just better fresh, and by fresh I mean ten minutes out of the garden. Tomatoes, certainly, warm and vine ripened. Melons. Salad greens.

Fresh is better, but just plain better is better too. You can grow a dozen different delicious salad vegetables that are too delicate to pack and ship. If you use Iceberg, when was the last time you used "delicious" to describe a lettuce? And there are so many varieties of tomatoes that taste so much better than whatever the supermarket carries, even in high season.

The seed catalogs are arriving now. Take a look.

The second reason they give is that it is good, low impact exercise. We're going to skip right past that one. It's true, but I don't want to think about it. I like to spade because it is enjoyable in some perverse way. If it's exercise, it loses its allure. Still, if thinking of it as good exercise will cause you to get rid of the rototiller, think away.

Three is garden to add beauty. True enough, but they miss the pith of it. It is true that gardening, even bad gardening, can add beauty to our homes. And that's good enough. They fail to mention, though, the competitive aspects of ornamental gardening.

There is great joy in making a good garden. There is greater joy in making a better garden, better than the neighbor's. Don't tell me you've never thought about that.

But that is not a bad thing in this case. You make a more beautiful garden than your neighbor, so the next year he makes an even

better garden. The following year you try harder, and the guy across the street joins the fray. Before long, the entire neighborhood is looking great. I've seen it happen.

Fourth is gardening to learn. Oh, come on. I know too many people who have been gardening for decades and haven't learned a thing.

The concept is good, though. I started out knowing nothing, but I have a compulsive curiosity, so now I know a little more than nothing. That's progress.

This winter pick five plants that you grow. Go to the library and look up everything you can find about them. You've got nothing better to do until February when you start the first seeds. Your five plants will appreciate it, and you might decide you want to know more about your other plants.

Number Five—garden to make money. Don't make me laugh. I'm a garden writer; I know better.

The one possible place where gardening can make you some decent money is if you are selling your house. A good landscape adds value in excess of the cost. But don't go overboard. A fantastic connoisseur's garden lowers the value. Potential buyers see work.

It goes on like that. These are not my reasons. If I can think of a good reason why I garden, I'll make a column out of it. Meanwhile I'm falling back on the mental disease thing.

DECEMBER

Bilko door

Float like a butterfly, sting like a bee. That's what Ali did to his opponents. And that's what winter did to me.

A lingering fall lulled me into thinking that winter would come on gently. Then——WHAM!—overnight we were in the Arctic. And—surprise!—I wasn't ready.

For one thing, the outside cellar entrance, which plays a major role in my winter regimen, was stuffed to the Bilko door with old kitchen cabinets, detritus of a kitchen remodel, which I intend to install for storage in the basement some day. They were in the stairwell because the bottom of the stairs was blocked with the old refrigerator, which I muscled that far and no further. I dreaded the massive job of clearing this jam. Which means I put it off.

Fortunately for me, our water heater broke. Clearing the cellar entrance, a project scheduled for sometime in the misty future, was rescheduled for RIGHT NOW.

A cellar stairwell, especially one with a leaky bottom door, is a valuable asset for any gardener. It stays dry and cold but not freezing. There is no better spot to force pots of spring bulbs. The temperature is perfect, and if you stick the pots in a garbage bag you only have to check them every six weeks to see if they need water. They probably don't.

The bulbs I potted up in November were still sitting on the back steps. Now frozen to the back steps. It isn't a good idea to let bulbs you are forcing freeze solid, but they will survive it, occasionally and briefly.

If you try to lift a pot that is frozen to the steps or deck, you will lift only part of it, usually leaving the bottom behind. The best way to get them free is to put a putty knife at the bottom edge and give it a light, a very light tap with a hammer. I know. I do this a lot.

If a pot is frozen to the ground, you need to stick a spade through the frost a couple of inches out from the bottom of the pot and lift it with the frost layer attached. Put it in the kitchen sink until the soil melts off. Do it when your wife isn't home.

The blitzkrieg of winter also froze the ground before I had planted all the bulbs I had bought. I could wait for the January thaw to plant them, or I could pot them up and put them in the outside cellarway. It is a little late for the larger bulbs like tulips, which need four months of cold, but it will work fine for crocus and grape hyacinths and other small and early bulbs.

The cellarway is also great storage for potted plants that are not quite hardy outside. Perennials safe in the ground in my Zone 5 garden are not hardy in pots. The soil in the pot will get much colder on bitter midwinter nights than the ground.

Though my garden is Zone 5, my cellarway is Zone 7, maybe even 8. Soon it will fill with pots of small shrubs and perennials. The beauty of this is that I can grow plants that are normally not hardy here. No more lusting over a picture in a catalog only to find the plant I fell in love with won't survive north of Virginia.

Since my cellarway has the climate, if not the ambiance, of the Carolinas, spring comes early. Flowering shrubs like azaleas are pushing out buds weeks before those planted outside.

I bring them up into the sunporch in February. It is colder than the house but warmer than outside, and they bloom in late March. It brings spring that much earlier.

With the cellarway full again, I should install the old cabinets as I intended. I'm going to get to that. Real soon.

Indoor Microclimates

It was one of those bright and bitter December days as we walked through the vacant house, heated just enough to keep water flowing in the pipes. I shivered as I pulled brittle newspaper from the cracks in a door leading onto an unheated sun porch, stepped through, and walked into June. Sun filled the coarsely finished room, boosting temperatures into the seventies. Though we didn't recognize it until later, the decision was made then and there.

That was fifteen years ago. Since then I've explored every microclimate of this Victorian vernacular. (A Victorian vernacular is a house built while Queen Victoria reigned, but too common to have a named style; another term is "old house.") A quirky heating system and windows that either rattle or bind depending on the season give me a range of temperatures mimicking the homelands of a variety of plants.

That original sun porch is Zone 8, plus or minus. Plus, because it doesn't actually freeze, and minus because it stays cool on overcast winter days, which is another way of saying most winter days. Nevertheless, it is an appropriate home for many plants hardy up to Georgia. Two ranks of windows facing south and west make it the warmest room in the house on a sunny winter afternoon.

At night an open connecting door keeps the frost out. A more trendy type would call it solar heating and install a fan thermostatically controlled to move warm air back and forth, but an open door does the job.

Hibiscus bought in four-inch pots now fill tubs on that porch. An eight foot pineapple guava guards the door and other subtropical trees and shrubs choke the room. Smaller pots sit on larger pots and line the windowsills. The cat once got lost in there for three days.

It's surprising how many plants we consider tender actually thrive in the chill. Geraniums, which grow soft and leggy in normal

indoor temperatures, stay tough and compact. Succulents that lingered for years as green oddities are now flowering plants. Many rhizomatous begonias put the lie to their tropical heritage; it's obvious that they love the lower temperatures. And an orchid cactus, admittedly ugly for 50 weeks each year, in March bursts into a spectacle that brings strangers knocking on the front door, even strangers without Bibles.

Visitors are drawn to this room, elbowing their way through the foliage to find a wicker chair, then pushing aside a lemon-laden branch or out-of-control jasmine to sit down. We felt the same when we moved in, gravitating at vespers to this unfinished space, once an open porch, closed in crudely like tens of thousands of them in the 1920's. Though there was much to do in this house that had not seen even new wallpaper since Truman, here was where we started.

It was easy and cheap. Two rolls of fern patterned paper covered the upper half of the two interior walls, blending with the porch ceiling fortuitously painted fern green. Quarter inch thick wainscoting, painted white, went around the bottom. A ceiling fan replaced the bare bulb in the center of the room. Three hundred bucks, a couple days' work, and we had a cozy spot for both plants and people.

Most of the people went away after dinner and brandy, but the plants stayed on and grew. Even if I never bought a new one (a laughable premise), plants that fit in the spring crowed in fall after a summer outside. Soon we were eyeing the open back porch off the kitchen. Rudimentary framing and patio door replacement panels, a fraction of the cost of real windows, soon gave us another space. We called it The Conservatory to avoid confusion, but it isn't really that pretentious.

Opened to the kitchen, the conservatory gave me Zone 9—Central Florida. Still cool at night, it was nonetheless balmier than the sun porch, and the south and east exposure warmed earlier in the morning. Now we had garden locations for both coffee and cocktails. Passion flowers that had sulked out front loved it, and a papaya was so grateful that it stopped dropping fruit with a midnight thump.

Both of these rooms are sad looking spaces in summer, but who cares. We're outside in summer, and so are the plants. A gravel patio in back. largely unplantable, turns tropical. Where you might expect only puny pots of petunias and geraniums, there are now figs and feijoas, agapanthus and crinums, guava and bananas, passion fruit climbing gleefully along a fence, sumptuous hibiscus. (Hibiscus were the one thing that made winter trips to Florida worthwhile. Now I don't have to go down there anymore, so the sun porch pays for itself.)

Even with this range of plants available to me, I find myself gazing wistfully at catalog illustrations of temperate climate plants too tender for my Zone 5 winters. In their zone 7 homeland, most were either herbaceous or deciduous. By the fall after the new Conservatory, space was already at a premium again, and I could not justify filling it with bare stems and seemingly empty pots. Besides, plants that hibernate need some cold—just not quite as much as my garden had to offer them.

I started probing new spaces, stretching my imagination and isolating zones with my maximum/minimum thermometer. The well house was Zone 7. The garage was still Zone 5, but more benign than my windswept hillside. An attached garage would be even more amenable, maybe Zone 7 against an outside wall, Zone 8 on an inside wall.

Then there was the cellar bulkhead entrance. No one hefts those doors from November to March, so there was all this wasted space. I found I could keep the temperature right around freezing by opening the connecting door into the cellar on the coldest nights. It is filled with plants that are hardy in the ground here but questionable when potted—lilies, lycoris, cosmos, and such.

Winter care for these diverse gardens is easier than main season gardening, but like powdered butter, it retains some of the flavor. Watering is minimal, since plants are either sleeping or at least

resting. The most arduous task is raking the leaves that drop daily, but even this has its benefits. After four decades, my wife and I sometimes run out of conversation, but if I neglect the fallen leaves for a few days, it gives us something to chat about.

The best part, though, is that I now leaf through the catalogs without the traditional bitter pill, where you are captured by a photo only to learn that the plant is too tender for your climate. No matter where they're suitable, Maine to Florida, I can find a place for them.

Winter Blooms

I have an old gardening book titled *Plants That Really Bloom Indoors* by George and Virginie Elbert. With due respect for a couple of revered garden writers, it's a joke. Maybe they bloomed for George and Virginie, but most of them don't bloom for me, certainly not in winter.

There are, however, some plants that do. Even for me. Maybe I should write a new book on the subject. But the sad fact is, I can probably cover them all in one column.

We'll quickly pass by the rug-weeds—African violets and poinsettias—without comment.

Regular readers know that one of my favorite winter flowers is the purple leafed shamrock, *Oxalis triangularis*. It is also one of my favorite summer flowers, but that's a story for another, warmer day (page 112).

If you had a pot of these outside for the summer, and it's still out there, it's probably not too late. Bring it in and knock it out of the pot. You'll find clumps of corms that look like grubs at an orgy. Break up the party and plant the individual corms into new soil, a couple inches apart. Keep it dry for the moment and wait. Before long little purple sprouts will start to grow. Put it in a bright window (direct sun is nice but not necessary) and water. You'll have flowers in January or February.

The flowers are lacy and pale. If you want big and bold, there is the ever-popular—and rightfully so—amaryllis. Amaryllis are idiot-proof. And if you have bought a new amaryllis and it failed to bloom, then...well, never mind. Embrace plastic.

I always buy a couple, wrap them in Christmas paper, and put them under the tree. If someone comes with an unexpected gift, I can pull one out—Oops, sorry, the tag fell off—and reciprocate. But I hope no one comes and I get to keep it myself.

I would prefer not buy amaryllis in boxed kits, complete with pot and soil, but they are easier to wrap and maintain the fiction. The loose bulbs in the crate are a better buy. They are bigger at the same price, and with amaryllis, bigger is better.

If you have an amaryllis that bloomed last year, and it is still green and growing, you need to practice tough love. Stop watering and let it die. Don't cut the leaves off. Let me say that again: DON'T CUT THE LEAVES OFF. Wait until they are dry and papery and come off with a gentle tug. Keep it dry until a bud appears in the neck. It will be later than last year, but it will bloom.

Easier, just as reliable—more reliable year after year—and even more dramatic is the clivia, and I am going to make one more plea for you to get one. They are pricey, I know, but this is an heirloom plant, one you will pass on to your children. Killing them takes a special talent.

They need almost no watering in winter, require very little light, and still throw a long lived, grapefruit sized blossom in bright orange. Just the thing you need in February.

If you go on the Internet to find a clivia, look for Veltheimia, too. They are different. While clivia has handsome broad strap leaves year round, an attractive foliage plant on its own, Veltheimia doesn't. Yes, it does have beautiful ruffled leaves, but they die back in late spring. The bulb aestivates, the opposite of hibernating; it goes dormant for the summer, not in itself a bad thing. You can throw it in the basement while you devote yourself to more important summer gardening.

What they have in common is reliable flowers in mid-winter. The veltheimia has a pink flower, like a pink red hot poker, on a sturdy 18-inch stem. And it multiplies, producing more stems each year.

There's Christmas cactus, of course. If you have one your grandmother passed on and it still blooms, you don't need any advice from me. If it doesn't bloom, keep it cool and make sure it doesn't get any artificial light after the sun goes down. And if you want something just as easy but more spectacular by orders of magnitude, look into orchid cactus.

For those who think flowers are something you have between Memorial Day and Labor Day and are content with that, ignore all of this. But if you think that flowers in January are something that might just possibly lift your spirits, get one of these. Or all of these.

Concrete Reinforcing Wire

You've seen the television commercials in muted gray, wordless, staccato violins that linger in your head. The shadow of a beautiful woman, the shadow of a handsome man, the glamorous gift, the grateful embrace.

You know right off these shadowy people are not gardeners. Gardeners don't want diamonds for Christmas. If you want to get that misty-eyed embrace from the gardener in your life, give her her very own roll of concrete reinforcing wire.

214

As a fringe benefit, you don't have to wash up, shave, dress, and go to one of those ritzy jewelry stores. You can shop for it at a building supply. A guy place. And it costs less than precious stones—50 to 70 bucks. The down side is that it is really hard to wrap. I wouldn't try anything more than a big red bow.

Concrete reinforcing wire is heavy duty wire welded into a roll that looks like five foot high fencing with six inch squares. It's used to strengthen concrete. For years gardeners have gotten what they could scrounge from Midnight Building Supply, a scrap here and there. But this stuff is so useful in the garden that it is worth having a whole roll.

It is universally accepted—universally in the room where I am writing this—that CRW makes the best possible tomato cages. Hack off a three foot piece from the roll (a hacksaw works, but bolt cutters are faster), form it into a cylinder, and hook it together with the six inch exposed nubs of wire. Cut off the bottom-most circle of wire to expose more six-inch stubs to push into the ground.

This will make a cage that will last for a decade or more. Eventually the bottom spikes break off. No problem. Cut off the next circle of wire and you have a cage six inches shorter that will last another decade.

But think beyond tomatoes. CRW tomato cages can save space and keep vining crops like cucumbers and Malabar spinach off the ground. And if you don't have any ground, put one in half of a plastic 55 gallon drum. (There's another gift idea, and junk yards have an even more casual dress code than building supply stores.)

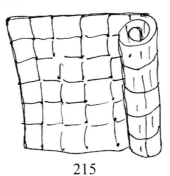

Tomato cages also have their place in the flower garden. Tall flowers prone to falling over, like delphiniums and dahlias, are easily supported. By early summer the plant has grown up through the cylinder and completely hidden it.

Not all flowers are tall. But one five foot cage can be cut in half to make two thirty-inch cages for peonies and such.

When you have a whole roll, you can be profligate in its use. I have an 18 foot row in my garden for melons, and down the middle runs a fence of CRW attached to steel stakes every six feet. It is strong enough to hold the vigorously climbing vines. And when a melon gets too big for its own good, I can slip it into a piece of worn-out panty hose and tie it to the wire.

Cut a long piece and bend it lengthwise for an ideal support for plastic tunnels and shade material. Much better and easier than hoops.

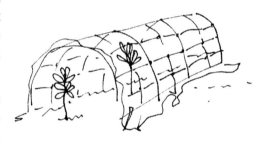

A scrap of CRW thrown on the soil surface is great for accurately spacing seeds and transplants. It divides the plot into six inch squares, four to the foot, which makes square foot gardening a cinch. Put four beet seeds in each square or one lettuce transplant. Larger crops like cabbage or peppers go in the center crossing of four squares, giving them one square foot each.

Small, closely spaced seeds like radish and carrots are easy, too. If you try to broadcast them over a large area, you know it comes out uneven, with clumps here and blank spots there. But if you plant one six-inch square at a time you get them just right.

I ask you, ladies, isn't this better than some useless gewgaw? Clip the column and tape it to the shaving mirror. No need to thank me.

Big Words

I collect words. It's a good hobby. Words are inexpensive, they don't take up a lot of space, and they don't need dusting.

Most of the words do not specifically relate to gardening. I can tell you that I divagate, but you already know that. Despite my pleonastic prolixity, I often suffer from lethologica, and I'd tell people that except that I can never remember the word.

Some have a dual purpose, useful both in the garden and in real life. Things that have a bloom, that is, a powdery covering, are pruinose. Grapes are pruinose; so are elderly aunts. Or take a geometry term like quincunx. Picture four dots forming a square, then add a fifth dot in the center. That is a quincunx. It's the perfect planting pattern in raised beds or wide rows.

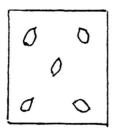

There is, however, a hefty pile of strictly hortulan words. In fact, hortulan is one. An old word fallen from favor, it means "relating to" or "of the garden." There is no current word that quite gets that job done, so we should revive hortulan. Work it into your conversation today.

Some words confer instant though often misplaced hortulan experthood (pardon my neologism). Asked to diagnose an ailing house plant, I may give it a lengthy examination and pronounce that it suffers from necrosis. This just means that it has dead leaves, but it seems to satisfy most.

Or perhaps it just suffers from etiolation, a bleached-out look caused by lack of light. If you have ever bought a deathly pale left-over amaryllis that had grown and bloomed in its box, you have seen etiolation. Of if you ever ate celery or cauliflower.

If you talk to your houseplants, there are several things I would presume about you. One of them is that you believe in floromancy. That is the view that plants have sentience. I often doubt whether even gardeners have sentience.

Everyone knows that one piece of a fern is a frond. Not everyone knows that one piece of bamboo is a culm, but now you do. If you have any growing near you, though, you well understand that the concept of one piece of bamboo is purely an abstraction.

Would you eat something that was acetarious? Of course you would. Acetarious vegetables are those used in salads. Before you eat them, clean off the frass. Frass is—well, it's bug poop. There is a word for everything.

Resting in the rafters of your garage you may have a rope-operated pruner on a long pole. If you do, you have an averruncator. I'll bet you didn't know that. Sometimes people mistakenly call it an aberuncator; be sure to correct them.

Some back to nature types may also have a scythe in the barn. If they do, I hope they also have a snath or they're going to have trouble. A scythe is the metal blade, and to wield it you need a snath—the handle.

Some plants in your garden, like azaleas, may be tropophilous, yet have specific edaphic requirements. Huh?! Tropophilous plants are those that adjust to changing climates. And edaphic means "relating to the soil." You could say they'll take the temps if the soil is right, but that wouldn't be as much fun.

I have always wanted to write a column on phenology, but I've never been able to assemble enough material. Phenology is the study of timing garden tasks with observable natural phenomenon. For example, you plant peas when the crocus bloom and set out broccoli when you hear the first lawn mower. There is something you do when oak leaves are the size of mouse ears, but I forget what it is.

But enough of this sciolism. I have more, but my spell checker is starting to smoke. And there's enough here already to make you completely incomprehensible.

Small Words

I have been told that my stuff can be...well...hard to grasp at times. The truth is that I seek out the right word, which may be a big word, but a word that lets me say just what I mean. If some are words you don't know, though, it's not much help to you.

So I will write here a plain, down to earth guide on how to care for house plants. (I thought that was one word, but my Spell Check tells me it is two.) A child could get it.

House plants are not hard to cope with if you give them what they want. If you try to get them to do what YOU want, though, you will fail.

So you buy a house plant. The first call is where to put the thing. Don't place it on a stand in a dark room next to the heat vent. You may want it there, and it may look good there, for a time, but it will die. Plants need light. Plants that are said to get by with dim light still need light. Dim does not mean dark. They may take it for a while, but they won't thrive and they won't live long.

At this time of year most plants like to have more than just bright light. They want to have rays of sun hit them smack on the leaf. A plant that might be burned by too much sun in June will take all it can get now. They want to be near glass, not in some dark niche at the back of the room.

And heat vents are death. They dry the air for one thing; most plants like moist air. And they make drafts, which can dry a plant more. Plus, of course, they get too hot.

Now comes the hard part. House plants do not like to be wet all the time. That is the one thing that kills more plants than any lapse in care. But they don't like to be bone dry for a long time. This can vex you if you are new at the job.

The rule is to wait till the soil is dry, not just the top but at least an inch deep. Don't take a glance and move on. Touch it, feel it. Or lift the pot. A dry pot is light, a wet pot has some heft. When it has dried, drench it. Then wait till it dries out once more.

When do you do this? Well, what kind of plant do you have? How big is the pot? What time of year is it? A plant that dries in two days when it's hot and bright may go two weeks or more when it is cool and dim. A plant in a small pot wilts while one in a large pot is still wet. As I said, feel it.

In short, check them each day and tend them when they need it, not on some hard and fast plan. Don't fret. You'll learn. It just takes time. Time, and a few dead plants.

For the most part plants don't need as much food as we think. They need none at all in the cold months. None. When it warms up and they start to grow once more, get a small jar of house plant food and use half of what it tells you to. Half will do the job and it won't burn the plant.

From time to time you may need to put your plant in a new pot. When roots come out the hole in the pot, it's time. Pull it out of the old pot and get a new one just one size up. Don't get a huge pot. Put some soil in the base, plunk in the plant, and stuff new soil down the edge. Tamp it down so there are no air holes. Not much to it.

Soil is key. Don't use soil from your yard. And don't buy the dark brown "dirt" at ten pounds for a buck. (Dirt is what you wash off your hands; soil is what you grow plants in.) Get a bag of peat based soil mix. Fake soil, or *faux* soil as they say on the tube. It will cost a bit more, but you save in the long run since you won't have to buy new plants all the time.

And there you have it. Short and to the point. You can't gripe that this is too dense. Not a word here has more than one syllable.

Oops.

INDEX

221

For more information about this book and other titles from
B. B. Mackey Books, go to www.mackeybooks.com or
email betty@mackeybooks.com.

223

Breinigsville, PA USA
08 December 2010
250909BV00003B/43/P